# The Natural Lunchbox

## Vegetarian Meals for School, Work & Home

### Judy A. Brown

Book Publishing Company
Summertown, Tennessee

Cover Design: Beverly Lacy, Cynthia Holzapfel
Interior Design: Jerry Hutchens, Cynthia Holzapfel

Book Publishing Company
PO Box 99
Summertown, TN 38483
888-260-8458

17  16  15  14  13  12  11  10  09  08        10  9  8  7  6  5

ISBN-13:  978-1-57067-026-8
ISBN-10:  1-57067-026-9

Brown,  Judy A.
     The natural lunchbox  :  vegetarian meals for school, work, and home   /  Judy A. Brown
          p.   cm.
     Includes index.
     ISBN  1-57067-026-9  (alk. paper)
     1.  Vegetarian cookery.  2.  Lunchbox cookery.  I.  Title.
     TX837.B867  1996
     641.5'636–dc20                                        96-18107
                                                                CIP

Book Publishing Co. is a member of Green Press Initiative. We chose to print this title on paper with postconsumer recycled content, processed without chlorine, which saved the following natural resources:

| | | |
|---|---|---|
| 618 pounds of solid waste | | 4,813 gallons of water |
| 1,159 pounds of greenhouse gases | | 13 trees |
| | 9 million BTU of energy | |

For more information, visit <www.greenpressinitiative.org>. Savings calculations thanks to the Environmental Defense Paper Calculator, <www.papercalculator.org>.

Calculations for the nutritional analyses in this book are based on the average number of servings listed with the recipes and the average amount of an ingredient if a range is called for. Calculations are rounded up to the nearest gram. If two options for an ingredient are listed, the first one is used. Not included are fat used for frying, unless the amount is specified in the recipe, optional ingredients, or servings suggestions.

# A Tribute to My Mom and Dad

This book, (like my first book *Judy Brown's Guide to Natural Foods Cooking*) along with all the work I do in the natural foods industry and have been doing for the last 20 years, is dedicated to my Dad, Everett Brown. It was my Dad's seven-year battle with cancer and eventual death that inspired me to research, to change my diet and lifestyle, and to pursue the work I am committed to today. I would also like to acknowledge my Mother, Delores Brown, and thank her for her support, her love, her strength, and her superior example of a role model as she grew strong and went on with her life after my Dad's passing. (You would have to know just how wonderful and special my Dad was as a person, a father, and a husband, to understand how difficult this would be.)

In my commitment to whole foods, I have believed that it was my Dad's illness that was the main impetus for my work. But after years of soul searching, I've realized that growing up with a mother who devoted her life to her family, who was a homemaker, and who put a tremendous amount of energy into providing well-balanced, nutritious home-cooked meals has also been a major inspiration for me. We always had lots of variety, fresh fruits and vegetables, and rarely ate out. We always had three excellent meals a day.

Every Monday night in our house was Soul Night. Soul Night consisted of pinto or navy beans, kale or collards, turnips, rice (in latter years brown rice), and corn bread. And I mean every Monday night without fail!

Even though we were a Navy family that moved around most of my life, Soul Night was the connection to our Southern heritage, since my Mom was from Mississippi and my Dad from Kentucky. (Try my Aunt Linda's Squash Casserole and Baked Beans. They are delicious.) Little did my Mom realize the groundwork she was setting for my eventually becoming a vegetarian. That meal has grown with me through the years and has been a natural part of my transition to a vegetarian diet. To this day, that is still my favorite meal.

I have tried my best to make this a good book with tasty, nutritious, and, as much as possible, low-fat recipes. I have tried to perfect each and every recipe, but you must realize that I have created these recipes according to my taste buds. I hope this book will serve as a guide and that you will add your creativity and tastes to the recipes.

# Contents

# Foreword

We are on the go nowadays, more than ever before, and that can present a challenge if you want to eat healthful foods. Lunch might come from our desk drawer or from a brown bag between classes. And at home, picky eaters—young and old—may not always share our enthusiasm for healthful foods.

The Natural Lunchbox is full of delightful treats to answer these and just about every other hurdle you will ever come across. Judy Brown is a creative cook and an innovative instructor. She is at her very best in showing the why's and how's of eating for health without sacrificing convenience.

Perhaps most importantly, Judy Brown has never forgotten that, while we want the very best foods for our arteries, our waistlines, and every other part of us, every bite touches our taste buds first. Her creations are as delectable as they are health supporting, with endless choices for every possible taste.

I hope you enjoy the practical information you will find here, and the delights that Judy''s wonderful recipes have in store for you.

NEAL D. BARNARD, M.D.

# Acknowledgments

There's a lot of talent that has come together in developing this book. My heartfelt thanks goes out to all the individuals and companies who have contributed ideas and recipes and who believe, as I do, in the value of a vegetarian, whole-foods-based diet. I could not have done this book without their contributions.

I would like to thank Mimi Clark, a vegetarian cooking instructor in Northern Virginia, who contributed, and assisted in developing, a number of the recipes. Her dedication, motivation, friendship, and sense of humor came at a desperately needed time. Thanks are due to Eric Gordon, Director of Training at Fresh Fields and graduate of the New York Natural Gourmet Cookery School, Jeff McDonald, for his favorite salad dressing, and my California friend, Maureen Burns, for her idea for Maureen's Healthy Grains. Carrie Irre deserves praise for her countless ideas and inspiring interest in cooking. Thanks to David Hawkins for his favorite flax dressing and sandwich recipe. He is a special friend and owner of Mother Earth Foods, the oldest natural foods store in West Virginia. Thanks also to his mother, Eva Hawkins, a long time natural foods advocate for her tasty and nutritious recipe ideas. I also want to thank Maine Coast Sea Vegetables, natural food manufacturer, who provided their popular recipe for the book. I am so thankful that these individuals and companies believe enough in me to contribute to this book.

I especially want to thank the Book Publishing Company for their patience and support. A special thanks to Cynthia Holzapfel and Michael Cook for their editing.

I want to thank my Mom, my sister Debbie, my vegetarian counselor Betsey, and all of my friends and relatives for being there for me.

Lastly I want to thank my daughter Cheyenne for being such a good eater and helping mommy eat the recipes as they were being tested. Her discerning taste buds helped me with many recipes. Some of her favorites are the Seasoned Greens, Seasoned Arame, and Garlic Brussels Sprouts.

"A good cook is like a sorceress who dispenses happiness," Elsa Schiaparelli, Shocking Life

# Planning Your Lunches
## Keep Leftovers In Mind

It was once said, "Breakfast like a king, lunch like a prince, and dinner like a pauper" (Anonymous). Lunch is an important meal that is often overlooked because of our hectic schedules.

A lot of people eat on the run and utilize fast food to get them through the day. This book is written with the hopes of providing tasty, nutritious, vegetarian-oriented, sometimes quick, sometimes hearty dishes for brown bagging it—lunches you can eat at work, school, on the road, or at home.

Why go to the trouble to make your own lunch? For one thing, it is definitely economical—it will save you money in the long run. You have control over what you are eating and how it is prepared. You know what is in the food you are eating. You can eat it anytime and anywhere you want. Making your own lunches insures their nutritional value and can help limit the fat, cholesterol, and excess salt and sugar in your diet.

The best way to be sure that you and your family will eat healthfully is to try as much as possible to plan ahead for your meals and snacks. Keep a list on the refrigerator to add to every time you think of something you need. If you can, consider setting aside half an hour or more a week to think of the next weeks menu and put a shopping list together. Try to keep variety in the diet as much as possible, and try new things on a regular basis.

Try to cook with the thought of leftovers in mind. When deciding to prepare a recipe, consider how much you want to make. Do you want it to last for one or two meals, or do you want significant leftovers to spread out through the week? Consider doubling or tripling the recipe you are preparing.

Buy foods you can make which are especially good as leftovers—beans and grains are great reheated for lunch. All types of salads containing vegetables, grains, and beans are easy because they can be eaten as is. Soup is always good for lunch, along with stews, and casseroles. Stir frys are another good idea for lunch. Dishes, such as lasagne, are filling and are very tasty reheated.

Protein at lunch time can help you stay alert in the afternoon. Emphasize soy-foods (such as tofu or tempeh) beans, nuts, seeds, and grains.

Take into consideration your own criteria for eating—can you eat anything hot or cold, or do you need foods that are usually served hot to be warmed up? If that is the case, you either have to have a microwave or heating element at work, carry a thermos, or stick with salads, sandwiches, and dips for lunch.

When I think about lunches, I can't help but think about a roommate I had in California, named Larry, who was macrobiotic. Once a week he went into major production preparing a variety of burritos for next week's lunches. He would make two to three different fillings for the burritos, then he would fill them, roll them, and wrap each one individually with plastic wrap. He would then place the burritos of the same kind in a large food storage bag, label them, and freeze them. Each day he would take out one or two from the freezer, and put them right into his lunch bag. His dedication and discipline was very inspiring.

## Planning for Your Lunches to Avoid the Fast Food Track

If you can get into the habit of planning ahead for lunches and making quantities that will last a few days, you can avoid the trap of grabbing food on the run, junking out, and eating fast food. Not only are these foods a strain on the pocketbook, if eaten regularly they are also a threat to your waistline and health. They don't necessarily contribute to that good, steady energy level and "feel-good feeling" you get after a wholesome meal that can carry you through the rest of your afternoon.

Here is a simple example to think about. A 4 oz. plain baked potato contains only 79 calories. Three ounces of french fries have 233 to 275 calories and approximately 11 to 14 gm. of fat. One ounce of potato chips has 150 calories and 9 gm. of fat.

"Great spirits have always encountered opposition from mediocre minds"

Albert Einstein

# Fat and Calories From Popular Fast Foods

Triple Cheeseburger—828 calories, 50 gm. fat

Double, triple, or jumbo burgers—680 calories, 9 teaspoons or 39 gm. fat

Fried chicken sandwiches—688 calories, 9 teaspoons or 40 gm. fat

Egg sausage biscuit or croissant sandwich—585 calories, 9 teaspoons or 40 gm. fat

Tuna fish sandwich w/mayo—566 calories, 28 gm. of fat

# Sugar Content of Popular Foods

Soda is the largest single source of sugar in the American diet.

12 oz. orange soda—11.8 teaspoons sugar

12 oz. cola soda—10 teaspoons sugar

½ cup jello—4½ teaspoons sugar

1 slice apple pie—7 teaspoons sugar

½ cup sherbet—9 teaspoons sugar

Here are some of the favorites that parents give their kids:

8 oz. Hawaiian punch—6½ teaspoons sugar

8 oz. Kool-Aid (you add sugar)—6⅓ teaspoons sugar

8 oz. Kool-Aid, sugar already added—5½ to 6 teaspoons sugar

1 popsicle—4½ teaspoons sugar

1 cup low-fat fruit yogurt—7½ teaspoons sugar

4 oz. whole milk frozen yogurt—6 teaspoons sugar

# Brown Bagging Tips
## (Nutritious Lunch Box Tips)

Believe it or not, there is a Brown Bag Institute in Green Farms, Connecticut. David Lyons, founder of the Institute, says that more than 34 million Americans tote their lunches to work or school each day, and half of all households have at least one brown bagger in the family. (Shape, Sept. 1987, p.44) Here are some suggestions to make your brown bagging a little easier.

* Pack appetizing foods for school lunches—ones that your children are interested in and will be comfortable eating around other children.

* For children, you may want to keep the portions small to avoid waste. Limit most portions to ½ cup. A half of a sandwich may be plenty for a child. A few slices of a pear or an apple may have a better chance of being eaten. A whole fruit may just end up in the trash. Consider providing miniature vegetables and fruits such as Belgian carrots, little corn, etc.

* Pick foods that your child likes. Test new foods at home before including them in their lunch box. Remember that children like repetition.

*Allow your children to get involved in lunch planning. Encourage them to offer you suggestions and help in packing the lunches. Is there something other kids eat that they would like to eat and that you could make in a nutritious way?

* Find out what's being served at school for the week. Maybe you can make similar items, such as pizza, lasagne, tacos, etc. but with natural ingredients.

* Use fun lunch boxes and take the time to hide little notes to your children that they will discover during their lunch. Turn your child's paper lunch bags into wild animals. Draw for your child (or have them draw) eyes, noses, mouths, and ears. They can cut out a face and glue it to the bottom of a paper bag. When they are done with their lunch they can have a wild animal puppet.

* Place stickers on plastic bags and food containers to draw your child's attention.

* Be sure to provide a protein source with each meal. It will help to keep your child awake in the latter part of the day. Protein is available in soy products, grains, beans, nut butters, nuts, and seeds.

* Always try to provide a vegetable with every lunch. Important nutrients and good eating habits are reinforced with steamed or raw carrot sticks (see recipe for Crinkle Carrot Fries page 151), stuffed celery sticks, sautéed zucchini, steamed broccoli with a dipping sauce, sliced cucumbers (remove the skin, especially if they are waxed), etc. My little girl, Cheyenne, will eat almost any vegetable if she has a dip such as hummus or tofu mayonnaise to dip it in. Her popular phrase is "I need more dip it." Vegetables hidden in soups and casseroles are a good way to get them in your child's diet.

* Don't pack the same foods every day—rotate foods to provide variety.

*Pack lunches to keep cold food cold and hot food hot.

* To avoid soggy sandwiches, keep the filling in a separate container. Keep fillings such as tomatoes, lettuce, and sprouts packed separately so they can be added to the sandwich just before eating.

* Consider preparing lunches the night before and keeping them in the refrigerator until you are ready to leave.

* Try to vary the tastes and textures of the foods. Pack something colorful, something crunchy, and something soft.

* Use aseptic packages of fruit juice and soy or rice milk for lunch boxes. They can be frozen the night before, and by lunch time they will be thawed out and cold to drink. Freeze soy malteds, cut off the top of the packages, and push up for a fun popsicle.

* Utilize the lunch box sizes of natural, unsweetened applesauce. There are also unsweetened, natural, sugar-free, non-dairy puddings that come in a variety of flavors. They can also be frozen the night before and will help keep the other food cold during the morning.

* Complete the lunch box meal with a treat—a sugar-free cookie, muffin, or fresh fruit. Other ideas are stuffed dates with almond or other nut butters and crispy brown rice. Stuff celery sticks with nut butters alone or nut butters mixed with mashed banana and topped with seeds, such as sunflower seeds. Make your own filled crackers by filling with nut butters or soy cream cheese.

# Quick Lunch and Leftover Ideas

* Dice up tofu hot dogs, and add them to your favorite baked beans or Aunt Linda's Baked Beans (page 64).

* For a quick chili, mix canned beans, (black beans or kidney beans), mash some with the liquid, and add corn and chopped tomatoes. Top with grated soy cheese. Heat up and pack in a thermos.

* Pack a pita sandwich with leftover salad, and add your favorite dressing. It's best if the dressing is transported in a small container and added just before eating. For a variation, add grated carrots, raisins, chopped nuts, and tofu mayonnaise or soy cream cheese.

* Keep whole wheat chapatis in the refrigerator for quick roll-up sandwiches. You can fill them with leftover salad ingredients, stir frys, beans and bean dips, soy cheese, sprouts, vegetarian patés, and soy cream cheese. The possibilities are unlimited. Cheyenne's favorite burrito is filled with vegetarian refried beans, shredded lettuce, leftover brown rice, chopped tomatoes, and mock or real guacamole.

* Use your dinner leftovers. Cold grains and pasta noodles can easily be turned into salads with the addition of raw or steamed vegetables, and beans.

* Here is a quick, homemade, cup-of-soup idea from Shape Magazine (Sept. 1987). Mix 2 tablespoons dried vegetables, vegetable based mock chicken broth seasoning, ¼ cup couscous, and herbal seasonings. Add water and let steep for 5 minutes.

* At the beginning of the week, prepare your favorite salad ingredients, such as grated carrots, shredded lettuce and cabbage, sliced cucumbers, chopped broccoli, etc., and keep in storage bags. This makes it easy to throw together a quick salad.

* Prepare a favorite pasta or two at the beginning of the week and keep in storage bags. Throw the pasta together with salad vegetables and your favorite dressing, or add to stir fried vegetables. Have cooked linguine or fettuccini on hand, ready to be reheated and served with spaghetti sauce.

* Boiled winter squash can be added as a fat substitute in baked goods. You can use squash or pumpkin puree to replace up to ¾ of the fat in muffins, quick breads, and cakes.

* Spread Black Bean Chili (page 63) between 2 heated corn tortillas, and top with salsa, chopped tomatoes, and cilantro.

* Canned beans can be added to salads, pasta dishes, stir frys, and soups for added protein.

# Sneaky Ways To Slip Nutrition Into Your Child's (or Picky Adults) Diet

* Is your child a picky eater? Try naming a recipe after them and see if that doesn't inspire them to try it.

* For added nutrition, add nutritional yeast (Red Star is the only brand made without whey) into casseroles, stews, and soups.

* Mix pureed vegetables into loaves, muffins, burgers, and pasta.

* Mix grated vegetables into pancakes, spreads, dips, and macaroni and cheese.

* All kinds of vegetables can be added to spaghetti sauce, such as steamed broccoli, zucchini, carrots, green and red peppers, onions, and green beans. They can be left chunky for kids who will eat them. Puree them for picky eaters.

* Add steamed and pureed vegetables such as butternut, acorn, and summer squash to macaroni and cheese or lasagne. It is best to puree them in a food processor or a blender. Start with a small amount until your kids get use to the taste. These vegetables add Vitamin A and other valuable nutrients and look like cheese in the dish.

* Add whole grains, such as barley and brown rice, to your favorite dishes to increase the fiber content. Cook the barley or brown rice ahead of time. You can keep it in the refrigerator for one week, or longer in the freezer. Add ⅓ cup of the grain to every serving of salad, pasta sauce, or soup.

* Freeze fruit-flavored soy yogurt and fruit-based smoothies (page 132) in popsicle molds.

* Mimi Clark's daughter, Sasha, rejects many foods and dishes in their whole form. Mimi's secret to get Sasha to eat them is to puree the food, spread it on ¼ of a pita bread, sprinkle it with some soy cheese, broil it, and call it pizza!

* Children like different pasta shapes. You can find pasta made for special occasions such as hearts, Christmas trees, Easter bunnies, etc. There are also bow ties, spirals, wagon wheels, shells, and alphabet pasta.

# Stocking A Whole Foods Kitchen

What are good things to have on hand in your kitchen in order to put together nutritious, delicious, sometimes quick, lunch meals? A well-stocked kitchen would include:

## Basic Grains
Brown rice
  short, medium,
  or long grain
Quinoa
Millet
Bulgur
Spelt
Amaranth
Barley
Wheat
Oats
Couscous

## Basic Legumes
Pinto Beans
Kidney Beans
Garbanzos (chick-peas)
Lentils
Black Beans
Navy Beans
Black-eyed peas

## Basic Condiments
Mustard
Ketchup—sugar free
Soy sauce—natural
  tamari or shoyu
Brown rice or apple
  cider vinegar

Balsamic vinegar or
  umeboshi vinegar
Mirin (rice cooking
  wine)
Sea salt
Herbal seasonings
Tofu Mayonnaise
Miso

## Basic Cooking Aids
Arrowroot powder
Egg replacer

## Cooking Oils
cold pressed (no heat
treatment, please)
  Canola oil
  Extra virgin olive oil
  Toasted sesame oil
  Canola spread
  Flax oil

## Vegetables
Carrots
Onions—yellow and red
Potatoes
Sweet potatoes, yams,
  winter squash
Summer squash yellow
  and zucchini

Greens—broccoli,
  kale, collards, green or
  red swiss chard,
  mustard greens
Cucumbers
Sprouts
Red, yellow, or green
  peppers
Cabbage—green and
  red

## Fruit
Apples
Bananas
Grapes
Fresh fruit in season—
  peaches, nectarines,
  blueberries, melons,
  strawberries
Dried fruit—figs,
  dates, prunes, apricots,
  etc.

## Packaged Food Items
Small packages - natural,
  sugar-free apple sauce
Small packages - natural,
  sugar-free puddings

# Scrumptious Sandwiches,
# Better Burgers,
# and
# Satisfying Spreads

# Powerhouse Sandwich

Yield: 4 sandwiches

½ pound tempeh, sliced in 4
  pieces, or 4 commercial
  veggie burgers of your choice

8 slices multi-grain bread

3 tablespoons soy mayonnaise
  (about 1 teaspoon per slice)

4 slices soy mozzarella cheese

4 slices tomato

4 cups clover or alfalfa sprouts

4 pieces Romaine lettuce

herbal seasoning to taste

**Steam** the tempeh for 20 minutes. Coat a large skillet with cooking oil spray, and brown the tempeh. (If you are using veggie burgers, cook according to package directions.)

**Spread** the bread with the mayonnaise, and top 4 slices with the tempeh, cheese, tomato, sprouts, lettuce, and seasoning.

**Cover** with the remaining slices of bread, slice in half, and serve with crisp, dill pickle spears.

Per sandwich: Calories: 318, Protein: 17 gm.,
  Fat: 11 gm., Carbohydrates: 38 gm.

*About this recipe*——

Here's the perfect sandwich for hearty appetites or anyone who thinks a vegetarian meal isn't satisfying!

# Open-Faced BLTs
# (Burger, Lettuce, & Tomato)

Serves 4

**Divide** the mustard between the bread slices, spread, and top with the lettuce.

**Top** with the rest of the ingredients. For brown bagging, wrap the sandwich in plastic wrap, but pack the tomatoes separately and add just before eating.

Per serving: Calories: 123, Protein: 5 gm., Fat: 3 gm., Carbohydrates: 16 gm.

*About this recipe—*

This is a delicious, calorie-conscious version of the traditional lunch-time favorite.

4 tablespoons Dijon mustard

4 slices whole grain bread

4 leaves Romaine lettuce

1 large tomato, cut in 4 slices

1 Vegetable Tofu Burger (page 25), crumbled, or 1 commercial veggie burger, crumbled

2 cups alfalfa or clover sprouts

# Quick & Easy Sloppy Joes

Serves 4

**Defrost** and press out the excess liquid from the tofu, and slice it into thin strips and pieces.

**Add** the barbecue sauce, heat, and pile into the buns.

Per serving: Calories: 280, Protein: 12 gm., Fat: 5 gm., Carbohydrates: 44 gm.

1 pound tofu, frozen

1 cup barbecue sauce of your choice

4 whole grain burger buns, warmed

*About this recipe—*

Lunch can be ready in 10 minutes with these

# Low-Fat Reubens

Yield: 4 sandwiches

2 cups Mock Guacamole
(page 32)

8 slices hearty, whole grain
bread

¼ cup drained sauerkraut

2 tablespoons soy mozzarella
cheese, grated (optional)

2 tablespoons Thousand Island
Dressing

**Spread** ½ cup of the Mock Guacamole on 4 slices of bread.

**Layer** the rest of the ingredients on top of the Mock Guacamole mixture, and top with 4 slices of bread.

**Lightly oil** a large skillet, and turn the heat to medium.

**Place** 2 sandwiches in the pan, and grill. If using soy cheese, place a lid on to help melt the cheese. Turn the sandwiches when brown on the bottom. Be careful they don't burn. This sandwich is also good ungrilled.

Per sandwich: Calories: 173, Protein: 9 gm.,
Fat: 3 gm., Carbohydrates: 27 gm.

# Veggie Roll Ups

Yield: 4 roll ups

4 whole wheat tortillas

1 cup Black Olive Spread
(page 36)

1 cup clover or alfalfa sprouts

4 pieces leaf lettuce, shredded

2 cup carrots, grated

**Lay out** the tortillas and spread ¼ cup of the Black Olive Spread across the middle of the tortilla.

**Top** each tortilla with ¼ cup alfalfa sprouts, ½ cup carrots, and lettuce, and roll up.

Per roll up: Calories: 209, Protein: 10 gm., Fat: 8 gm.,
Carbohydrates: 24 gm.

# Veggie Hero Sandwich

Yield: 4 sandwiches

**Cut** the french bread in half to the edge. Do not completely cut in half. Spread your favorite mustard across the top and bottom of the bread, and set aside.

**Mix** together the water, lemon juice, herbs, and salt in a small bowl.

**Place** the lettuce, cucumber, and green onions in a bowl. Pour the lemon juice mixture over all, and toss gently.

**Lay** the cheese across the bottom of the bread. Next arrange the soy deli meats, lettuce, cucumber mixture, and top with the tomatoes.

**Cut** into 4 sandwiches. Enjoy! For brown bagging, pack the lettuce, cucumber mix, and tomatoes separately.

Per sandwich: Calories: 306, Protein: 17 gm.,
   Fat: 11 gm., Carbohydrates: 34 gm.

1 loaf French Bread

2 teaspoons Dijon or honey
   mustard

1 tablespoon water

1 tablespoon fresh lemon juice

½ teaspoon basil

½ teaspoon oregano

½ teaspoon marjoram

½ teaspoon sea salt

2 cups romaine lettuce,
   shredded

1 large cucumber, chopped

2 green onions, sliced

2 tomatoes, sliced

4 slices soy bologna meatless
   deli slices

4 slices soy turkey deli
   slices

4 slices soy cheddar cheese

*Food for thought . . .*

Tell me what you eat, and I will tell you what you are.

—Antheleme Brillat Savarin

# Stuffed Round Bread

Serves 6

1 whole grain round bread

2 tablespoons soy mayonnaise

2 tablespoons mustard

3 to 4 large pieces of romaine
lettuce

3 roma tomatoes, sliced in
rounds

1 medium cucumber, peeled
and sliced

3 to 4 slices tofu bologna or
tofu, thinly sliced and sautéed

2 carrots, grated

1 cup clover or alfalfa sprouts

**Cut** the top off of the bread, scoop out the inside, and gently trim off the underside of the lid.

**Spread** the soy mayonnaise around the inside of the bottom of the bread.

**Spread** the mustard across the underside of the lid.

**Layer** the lettuce, tomatoes, cucumber, bologna, carrots, and sprouts.

**Place** the lid back on the top of the loaf, cut it into 6 wedges, and serve. If desired, you can season the vegetable layers with herbal seasoning. For brown bagging, keep the tomatoes separate, and add just before eating.

Per serving: Calories: 164, Protein: 6 gm., Fat: 5 gm., Carbohydrates: 22 gm.

## Did you know?

A 1987 National Academy of Sciences report estimated that pesticides might cause an extra 1.4 million cancer cases among Americans. Pesticides are also implicated in nerve damage, birth defects, and genetic mutation. Support organic agriculture.

# Stuffed Sandwiches

Yield: 4 sandwiches

**Sauté** the broccoli, onion, and peppers in the water in a large skillet, for about 10 minutes until tender. Use a slotted spoon to remove vegetables.

**Place** 1 cup of the vegetable mixture on top of each flat bread.

**Pour** about 2 to 3 tablespoons barbecue sauce on top of each sandwich, and mix in with the vegetables.

**Fold** the bread over and use a toothpick to hold the ends together.

Per sandwich: Calories: 162, Protein: 5 gm., Fat: 3 gm., Carbohydrates: 33 gm.

2 cups broccoli, chopped

1 small onion, cut in large slices

2 cups assorted yellow, red, and green peppers or frozen pepper stir fry

1 cup + 2 tablespoons water

4 pieces Italian flat bread, warmed

barbecue sauce to taste

## Did you know?

Broccoli (the wonder food) is high in Vitamin C and fiber and provides calcium, magnesium, iron, and folic acid.

# Zucchini & Red Pepper Muffaletta

Yield: 4 sandwiches

4 whole grain Kaiser rolls

1 green pepper, cut in strips

1 red pepper, cut in strips

1 small onion, cut in thin slices

2 teaspoons minced garlic (from a jar)

1 small zucchini, cut in strips

¾ cup mushrooms, sliced

½ teaspoon sea salt

½ teaspoon tarragon

¼ teaspoon black pepper

2 tablespoons red wine vinegar or balsamic vinegar

soy mozzarella, grated (optional)

**Cut** the Kaiser rolls in half, and scoop out the insides of the rolls.

**Spray** a large nonstick skillet with some olive oil spray, and sauté the peppers, onion, and garlic. Partially cover with a lid, and sauté about 8 minutes.

**Add** the zucchini and mushrooms, and sauté 5 more minutes until crisp tender.

**Add** the spices and vinegar, and cook on high heat until the liquid is evaporated.

**Stuff** each half of the Kaiser roll with the vegetable mixture. You can also sprinkle some soy mozzarella on the top of each half, and bake in a 350° oven for 15 minutes.

Per sandwich: Calories: 143, Protein: 5 gm., Fat: 1 gm., Carbohydrates: 28 gm.

*About this recipe——*

A muffaletta is a popular sandwich in New Orleans.

# Vegetable Tofu Burgers

Makes 8 burgers

**Preheat** the oven to 350°.

**Drain** and mash the tofu in a medium-sized mixing bowl, mix in the oats, and set aside.

**Spray** a small saucepan with canola spray, and sauté the onion for about 3 to 4 minutes until tender. Add to the tofu mix.

**Add** the red peppers, carrots, and tamari, and mix well.

**Use** a ¼ cup measuring cup to measure out each burger. Press and shape with your hands, and place on an oiled cookie sheet.

**Bake** for 15 minutes on one side, flip over, and bake for 10 more minutes.

½ pound firm tofu

¾ cup dry rolled oats

1 small onion, chopped

¼ cup marinated roasted red peppers, chopped

¼ cup carrots, grated

1 tablespoon tamari

Per burger: Calories: 64, Protein: 4 gm., Fat: 1 gm., Carbohydrates: 8 gm.

*Food for thought . . .*

The destiny of countries depends on the way they feed themselves.

—Antheleme Brillat Savarin

# Oat Burgers

Yield: 6 burgers

2 tablespoons egg replacer + ½ cup water

1 teaspoon minced garlic

1⅓ cups rolled oats

¼ cup red onion, chopped

1½ teaspoons vegetarian Worcestershire sauce

½ cup fruit-sweetened ketchup

½ cup cooked brown rice

brown rice flour

**Preheat** the oven to 350°.

**Mix** the egg replacer and water, and let set a few minutes.

**Mix** the garlic, oats, red onion, Worcestershire sauce, egg replacer mixture, ketchup, and brown rice flour In a large mixing bowl.

**Press** together into 6 good size burgers, coat with brown rice flour on each side, and place on a cooking pan or sheet coated with cooking oil.

**Bake** for 15 minutes on one side, turn over gently, and bake for another 10 minutes. Serve warm or cold. Great on a bun with lettuce, tomato, ketchup, and relish.

Per burger: Calories: 117, Protein: 4 gm., Fat: 2 gm., Carbohydrates: 24 gm.

## Did you know?

Water-soluble fiber, found in apples, dried beans, and oats, has been shown to help lower cholesterol in the blood.

# Spicy Lentil Patties

Yield: 12 patties

**Rinse** the lentils, add the water, bring to a boil, and reduce the heat.

**Add** the curry powder, coriander, cumin, and salt.

**Cover** the pan and cook 35 to 45 minutes until the lentils are tender. Set aside with the cover on.

**Preheat** the oven to 350°.

**Heat** a skillet and sauté the onion, carrot, and garlic in the olive oil.

**Drain** the lentils if necessary. Mash well and mix with the sautéed vegetables and bread crumbs.

**Mix** in the arrowroot and tomato paste mixture.

**Form** into balls and flatten into patties. Place on an oiled baking sheet, and bake for 40 minutes, turning the patties over half way through the cooking time. Serve on whole grain burger buns with all the trimmings.

Per pattie: Calories: 129, Protein: 6 gm., Fat: 1 gm., Carbohydrates: 23 gm.

1 cup lentils

3 cups water

1 teaspoon curry powder

1 teaspoon coriander

1 teaspoon cumin

pinch of sea salt

1 large onion, chopped

¼ cup carrot, finely chopped

2 cloves garlic, chopped

2 teaspoons olive oil

1½ cups whole grain bread crumbs

2 tablespoons arrowroot or cornstarch

2 tablespoons tomato paste mixed with 1 tablespoon light miso

## Did you know?

Lentils are a good source of complex carbohydrates, fiber, protein, and iron. They are easy to prepare and don't need to be soaked overnight like most beans.

# Black Bean and Salsa Cakes

Yield: 6 cakes

2¼ cups cooked black beans, rinsed and drained

4 tablespoons red onion, chopped

2 tablespoons sweet red pepper, chopped

2 tablespoons whole wheat pastry flour

2 tablespoons cilantro, chopped

1 teaspoon basil

2 teaspoons cumin

pinch of cayenne

½ teaspoon hot pepper sauce

2 slices soy mozzarella, cut into thirds

2 tablespoons Homemade Salsa (page 29)

**Mash** the beans with a fork, add the onion, red pepper, flour, cilantro, spices, and hot pepper sauce, and mix well.

**Moisten** your hands and form 6 cakes. Lightly oil a large skillet, and sauté 3 burgers at a time, pressing the burgers down a little with a spatula. Cook about 2 minutes on medium to medium-high heat.

**Turn over** and put a strip of soy mozzarella on top of each burger.

**Cover** the skillet with a lid, and cook 2 more minutes until the cheese is melted.

**Serve** warm and top each burger with salsa.

Per cake: Calories: 112, Protein: 6 gm., Fat: 1 gm., Carbohydrates: 18 gm.

# Pizza Burgers

Makes 6 burgers

**Steam** the tempeh for 20 minutes, drain, and cool.

**In a large skillet**, sauté the onion and pepper in the water until tender, about 8 minutes.

**Grate** the tempeh and add the onion and pepper.

**Stir** in the tamari and spices, and cook 5 minutes.

**Add** the tomato paste and cook 5 to 10 more minutes.

**Serve** between English muffins.

Per burger: Calories: 253, Protein: 13 gm., Fat: 4 gm., Carbohydrates: 40 gm.

½ pound tempeh

1 medium onion, chopped

1 green pepper, chopped

1-3 tablespoons water

2 tablespoons tamari

1 teaspoon oregano

1 teaspoon basil

½ teaspoon marjoram

¼ teaspoon red pepper flakes

1 (8 oz.) can tomato paste

6 whole wheat English muffins, split

# Homemade Salsa

Yield: 1½ cups

**Combine** all of the ingredients, and mix well.

Per 2 tablespoons: Calories: 5, Protein: 0 gm., Fat: 0 gm., Carbohydrates: 1 gm.

4 roma tomatoes, chopped

4 tablespoons red onion, chopped

2 tablespoons lemon or lime juice

3-4 tablespoons cilantro, chopped

pinch of sea salt

hot sauce or jalapeño peppers to taste

# Healthy Burger Buns

Makes 8 large buns

4 tablespoons sesame seeds

¼ cup warm water

1 tablespoon baking yeast

1 teaspoon barley malt syrup or honey

3-3½ cups whole wheat flour

1 cup water

½ teaspoon sea salt

**Preheat** the oven to 350°.

**Toast** the sesame seeds in a flat pan for 10 minutes in the oven. Remove and set aside. Turn the oven off.

**Combine** and let foam together ¼ cup warm water, the baking yeast, and barley malt syrup, in a large bowl.

**Stir** in the flour, 1 cup water, 2 tablespoons sesame seeds, and salt. Use your hands to mix as the dough gets stiff.

**Knead** for about 10 minutes on a lightly floured surface.

**Oil** a clean bowl and turn the dough around to coat with the oil. Cover the bowl with a warm damp towel, and let rise in a warm draft-free place until double in size.

**Press** the dough down and divide into balls. Flatten into ½-inch thick rounds. Press the remaining sesame seeds into the tops of the dough, and place, seed side up, on a lightly oiled baking sheet.

**Lay** a piece of waxed paper loosely over the top of the rolls, and let them rise until double in size.

**Preheat** the oven to 375°.

**Bake** for 16 to 18 minutes. Place on a rack to cool.

Per bun: Calories: 195, Protein: 7 gm., Fat: 2 gm., Carbohydrates: 35 gm.

# Hummus

Serves 6

**Cover** the garbanzo beans with water, and soak overnight. Drain and rinse.

**Place** the beans in a medium-size pot, and cover with the 6 cups water. Bring to a boil, lower the temperature to medium-high, and cook for about 1 hour until the beans are tender. Drain and reserve the liquid. (You can use leftover liquid for soup stock.)

**Place** the beans in a food processor or blender, and blend with 3 tablespoons of the bean cooking liquid, lemon juice, garlic, scallions, salt, and parsley.

1 cup garbanzo beans (chick-peas)

water for soaking

6 cups water for cooking

3 tablespoons cooking liquid

juice of 1 lemon

3 cloves garlic, minced

2 scallions, chopped

1 teaspoon sea salt

2 heaping tablespoons fresh parsley, chopped

Per serving: Calories: 94, Protein: 4 gm., Fat: 1 gm., Carbohydrates: 16 gm.

**Variation:** For a coarser texture, hand mash the beans, and add the scallions and garlic at the end. If you like the taste of tahini, you can add 2 to 4 tablespoons per recipe.

Per serving: Calories: 137, Protein: 5 gm., Fat: 5 gm., Carbohydrates: 18 gm.

*About this recipe—*

This makes a great sandwich spread, filling, or dip. Stuff it into pita bread with sprouts and cucumbers, or serve with warmed pita bread triangles or crackers

# Mock Guacamole

Yield: 2½ cups

1 (7 oz.) can asparagus spears, drained

½ (10 oz.) package frozen peas

2 tablespoons soy mayonnaise

2 tablespoons fresh cilantro, chopped

1 tablespoon fresh lime juice

1 clove garlic, minced

¼ teaspoon ground cumin

1 medium tomato, chopped

2 tablespoons red onion, chopped

**Puree** the asparagus, peas, soy mayonnaise, cilantro, lime juice, garlic, and cumin in a blender or food processor until smooth.

**Empty** into a small bowl, and add the tomato and onion.

**Season** to taste with the hot sauce of your choice. Serve the same day.

Per 2 tablespoons: Calories: 14, Protein: 1 gm., Fat: 0 gm., Carbohydrates: 2 gm.

*About this recipe——*

Guacamole is a delicious sandwich filling, burrito stuffer, etc., but it is loaded with fat. Here's a light and healthful alternative to enjoy.

*Did you know?*

It is best to cook asparagus with the tips up. This helps preserve the Vitamin C and B1. It is a good blood builder because of its chlorophyll content. Asparagus tips are high in Vitamin A.

# Lime Yogurt Guacamole

Serves 4

**Peal** and mash the avocados with a fork in a medium-sized bowl.

**Add** the yogurt, lime juice, oil, and seasoning, and stir well.

**Fold** in the pepper, celery, and onion. Chill and serve with Baked Pita Chips (page 128) or stuffed in pita bread with sprouts and grated carrots.

Per serving: Calories: 225, Protein: 4 gm., Fat: 16 gm., Carbohydrates: 15 gm.

**Variation:** Make your own Broccamole by substituting 1 to 2 cups broccoli that has been steamed, drained, and pureed for the avocado. Try the Broccamole with fresh lemon or lime juice, chopped tomatoes and onions, and fresh cilantro. It's a great snack idea.

Per serving: Calories: 101, Protein: 4 gm., Fat: 5 gm., Carbohydrates: 7 gm.

2 large ripe avocados

1 cup plain soy yogurt

2 tablespoons lime juice

1 tablespoon olive oil

1 teaspoon kelp/cayenne seasoning

¼ cup yellow pepper, diced

¼ cup celery, diced

1 tablespoon red onion, diced

*About this recipe——*

A special thanks to Maine Coast Sea Vegetables for this recipe.

# Tofu Cream Cheese

Yield: about 1 cup

¼ cup soaked cashews

1 cup extra firm tofu, drained

1 tablespoon + 1 teaspoon
     fresh lemon juice

2 teaspoons maple syrup

½ teaspoon sea salt

2 tablespoons water

**Soak** the cashews overnight in water, if possible, and drain.

**Drain** the tofu and press between paper towels to get rid of as much of the water as possible.

**Place** the tofu and the rest of the ingredients in the food processor. (You can use a blender, but a food processor works best.) Blend until smooth, stopping once to scrape the sides of the processor or blender.

**Keep** refrigerated. Use on bagels, muffins, or toast.

Per 2 tablespoons: Calories: 55, Protein: 3 gm.,
     Fat: 4 gm., Carbohydrates: 3 gm.

**Variation:** Make an herbed cream cheese by adding garlic, basil, marjoram, basil, thyme, chives, parsley, etc.

**Variation:** For a chutney spread, add ¼ cup of your favorite chutney and 2 tablespoons chopped pecans. Serve on crackers, Indian crackers, or with vegetables.

Per 2 tablespoons: Calories: 66, Protein: 2 gm.,
     Fat: 4 gm., Carbohydrates: 6 gm.

# Cashew Cheese

Yield: about 1 cup

**Place** the cashews and ½ cup water in a blender or food processor, and blend until smooth.

**Add** the lemon juice, nutritional yeast, and pimentos, and blend well.

**Heat** ½ cup water to a boil, and add the agar flakes and salt. Reduce the heat to low, and simmer for a few minutes until all the flakes are dissolved.

**Add** the agar mix to the cashew mixture, and blend again.

**Chill** for a few hours before serving.

Per 2 tablespoons: Calories: 62, Protein: 2 gm.,
    Fat: 5 gm., Carbohydrates: 5 gm.

½ cup cashews

½ cup water

1 tablespoon lemon juice

3-4 teaspoons nutritional yeast

2 oz. pimentos

½ cup water

1 tablespoon agar flakes

pinch of sea salt

*About this recipe——*

This is easy to make and comes out like soft cheese. It's a great snack with crackers or chips, or it can be stuffed in celery. Cashew Cheese also makes a good sandwich spread.

# Black Olive Spread

Yield: ¾ cup

1 cup extra firm tofu

1 tablespoon + 2 teaspoons
   fresh lemon juice

1¼ teaspoons soy sauce

2 teaspoons nutritional yeast

1 teaspoon water

¼ teaspoon garlic

¼-½ cup black olives, chopped

**Drain** and press the water out of the tofu.

**Place** the tofu along with the lemon juice, soy sauce, nutritional yeast, water, and garlic in a food processor or blender, and blend until smooth.

**Scrape** the tofu spread out of the processor or blender into a food storage container, and add the black olives. You can go lighter or heavier on the olives.

**Store** in the refrigerator. Serve on bagels, muffins, toast, sandwiches, whole wheat tortillas, and inside pita bread. Omit the olives for a variation on tofu cream cheese.

Per 2 tablespoons: Calories: 52, Protein: 3 gm.,
        Fat: 4 gm., Carbohydrates: 2 gm.

**Variation:** Add capers or pimentos to the olive spread.

## Did you know?

Olives are very high in potassium. Bernard Jensen, in his book Foods That Heal, recommends steeping 10 olives in a teapot of boiling water for a high potassium tea. He believes this will help keep the heart healthy.

# Tempeh Salad

Serves 4

**Spray** a medium-size skillet with canola mist, and sauté the tempeh on medium-low until browned, about 5 minutes.

**Add** the water, bay leaves, and tamari to the skillet, and cover with a lid, lower the heat to medium, and simmer for about 20 minutes until all the liquid is absorbed. Remove the lid and allow the tempeh to cool.

**In a small mixing bowl**, mix together the scallions, celery, parsley, relish, and tempeh.

**In a small bowl**, mix the tofu mayonnaise and mustard.

**Add** the dressing to the tempeh and vegetables, and mix well. Cover and chill before serving. You can also place the mixture in a food processor or blender to make a spread for crackers and sandwiches or to stuff cherry tomatoes, celery, or endive leaves.

8 oz. tempeh, cut in small
    cubes
¾ cup water
2 bay leaves
1 tablespoon tamari
2 scallions, chopped
1 stalk celery, chopped
¼ cup fresh parsley, minced
2 tablespoons natural relish
4 tablespoons tofu mayonnaise
2 tablespoons Dijon mustard
    with horseradish

Per serving: Calories: 175, Protein: 10 gm., Fat: 9 gm., Carbohydrates: 14 gm.

# Mock Chicken Salad

Serves 4

8 oz. chicken-style seitan

1 stalk celery, chopped

2 scallions, diced

¼ cup parsley, minced

2 tablespoons pickle relish

2-3 tablespoons soy mayonnaise

2 tablespoons nutritional yeast

2 teaspoons prepared mustard

1 teaspoon tamari

**Dice** the seitan into chunks.

**In a large bowl**, combine the seitan, celery, scallions, parsley, and relish.

**In a separate bowl**, combine the mayonnaise, nutritional yeast, mustard, and tamari.

**Combine** the seitan and dressing, and mix well. Refrigerate for at least 1 hour.

Per serving: Calories: 145, Protein: 21 gm., Fat: 2 gm., Carbohydrates: 8 gm.

# Eggless Egg Salad

Serves 4 to 6

16 oz. low-fat tofu, drained and mashed

2 stalks celery, diced

¼ cup red onion, diced

4 tablespoons tofu mayonnaise

¼ cup parsley, minced

1 teaspoon turmeric

1 teaspoon sea salt

2 tablespoons apple cider vinegar

**Mix** all of the ingredients in a medium-size mixing bowl.

Per serving: Calories: 91, Protein: 6 gm., Fat: 5 gm., Carbohydrates: 5 gm

**Variation:** Use 1 tablespoon umeboshi vinegar instead of the apple cider vinegar for a flavorful non-acidic version.

## About this recipe—

This can be used as a sandwich spread or a filling for pita bread, celery, and tomatoes.

*Succulent Salads,*
*Delicious Dressings,*
*and*
*Splendid Soups*

# Cole Slaw

Serves 8

½ green cabbage, shredded

½ red cabbage, shredded

2 carrots, shredded

¾ cup tofu mayonnaise

2 tablespoons apple cider
   vinegar or brown rice vinegar

2 teaspoons Dijon mustard

1 teaspoon maple syrup

**Shred** the cabbage and carrots, by hand or with a food processor, and mix together in a medium-sized mixing bowl.

**To make the dressing**, combine the tofu mayonnaise, vinegar, mustard, and maple syrup in a small mixing bowl.

**Pour** the mayonnaise dressing over the cabbage, and combine well. Chill and serve.

Per serving: Calories: 83, Protein: 1 gm., Fat: 5 gm., Carbohydrates: 8 gm.

**Variation:** Omit the Dijon mustard, substitute about 3 to 4 teaspoons umeboshi vinegar for the apple cider vinegar, and add 3 teaspoons lemon juice and 2 teaspoons maple syrup. You can also add roasted caraway, sunflower, or pumpkins seeds.

## Food for Thought . . .

Early to bed, and early to rise, makes a man healthy, wealthy, and wise.

—Benjamin Franklin

# Hearty Cucumber Tomato Salad

Serves 6

**Mix together** the cumbers, tomatoes, mozzarella, dulse, and cilantro.

**To make the dressing,** combine the water, vinegar, brown rice syrup, thyme, marjoram, and rosemary.

**Pour the dressing** over the vegetables, and mix well. Let set 30 minute in the refrigerator before serving, stirring occasionally.

Per serving: Calories: 43, Protein: 1 gm., Fat: 2 gm., Carbohydrates: 6 gm.

2 cucumbers, peeled and chopped

13 cherry tomatoes, chopped in half

¼ cup soy mozzarella, cut in cubes

¼ cup dulse, chopped (optional)

2 tablespoons cilantro

4 tablespoons water

5 tablespoons brown rice or apple cider vinegar

1 teaspoon brown rice syrup

1 teaspoon thyme

1 teaspoon marjoram

1 teaspoon fresh rosemary (optional)

*About this recipe* —

Cherry tomatoes and chunks of soy cheese add a distinctive touch to this traditional favorite.

# Carrie's Artichoke Salad

Serves 6

1 (16 oz.) package frozen petite peas

1 (14 oz.) jar water-packed artichoke hearts, drained and chopped

2 teaspoons garlic, chopped

3 tablespoons red onion, finely chopped

2 tablespoons + 1 teaspoon olive oil

1 tablespoon water

2 tablespoons brown rice vinegar

¼ teaspoon maple syrup

⅛ teaspoon marjoram

⅛ teaspoon tarragon

⅛ teaspoon basil

**Cook** the peas according to package directions, or allow them to completely thaw out, and drain.

**Add** the peas to the artichoke hearts, garlic, and red onion to a medium mixing bowl, and mix.

**To make** the dressing, combine the oil, water, vinegar, maple syrup, marjoram, tarragon, and basil.

**Add** the dressing to the vegetable mixture, and mix well. Chill before serving.

Per serving: Calories: 126, Protein: 4 gm., Fat: 6 gm., Carbohydrates: 15 gm.

## Did you know?

March, April, and May are the best months to buy fresh artichokes. Avoid the very large ones which tend to be tough. Artichokes are high in Vitamins C, A, iron, and calcium.

# Roasted Eggplant Salad

Serves 4 to 6

**Slice the eggplant** in half moons. Layer the slices in a medium bowl, and lightly sprinkle the layers with salt. This will reduce the bitterness of the eggplant. Weight down the eggplant with a lid or inverted plate, cover the slices with cold water, and set aside for 15 minutes.

**Preheat** the oven to 350°.

**Drain the eggplant** and rinse the slices well under running water. Arrange the slices on a baking sheet, and bake for about 30 minutes until tender.

**To make the dressing**, combine the vinegar, oil, water, mustard, garlic powder, and brown rice syrup in a small jar.

**While the eggplant is baking**, wash the lettuce, drain well, tear into bite-size pieces, and place in a medium mixing bowl.

**When the eggplant is tender**, add to the lettuce along with the walnuts.

**Mix the salad ingredients**. Shake up the dressing ingredients to re-combine well, and pour over the salad. Serve warm or at room temperature.

1 pound eggplant

⅓-½ cup balsamic vinegar

⅓ cup olive oil

⅓ cup water

½ tablespoon Dijon mustard

1 teaspoon garlic powder

½ teaspoon brown rice syrup
   or honey

1 head Romaine lettuce

¼ cup walnuts, chopped

Per serving: Calories: 195, Protein: 1 gm., Fat: 16 gm.,
   Carbohydrates: 9 gm.

*About this recipe——*

You can also use this salad as a filling for pita bread or tortillas.

# Mediterranean Vegetable Salad

Serves 6 to 8

1 pound extra-firm tofu, frozen

½ cup black olives, chopped

6 oz. water-packed artichoke hearts, drained and chopped

1 pound eggplant, chopped in 1-inch cubes

1 pound small red potatoes, cut in quarters

1 large red pepper, cut in 1-inch squares

1 large red onion, peeled and cut in wedges

8 whole cloves garlic, peeled

1 tablespoon olive oil

1½ teaspoons thyme

½ teaspoon marjoram

½ pound green beans, cut in thirds

2 tablespoons cup extra-virgin olive or flax oil

3 tablespoons water

4 tablespoons fresh lemon juice

4 teaspoons Dijon mustard

2 teaspoons brown rice syrup or honey

1 teaspoon fresh garlic, minced

pinch of sea salt (optional)

**Thaw the tofu** in the refrigerator overnight, under hot running water, or in the microwave on the defrost setting for several minutes. Squeeze out the excess moisture, drain well, and cut into ½-inch cubes.

**Mix the tofu** with the olives and artichoke hearts, and set aside.

**Preheat** the oven to 350°.

**Mix together** the eggplant, potatoes, red pepper, onion, and garlic, in a shallow baking pan.

**Sprinkle the vegetables** with 1 tablespoon olive oil, the thyme, and marjoram.

**Mix and bake** for about 60 minutes, stirring occasionally, until the potatoes and eggplant are tender.

**Steam the green beans** until crisp-tender, while the vegetables are baking.

**Cool the green beans** under cold water, and set aside, while the vegetables are baking,

**For a Dijon vinaigrette dressing**, combine two tablespoons olive oil, 3 tablespoons water the lemon juice, mustard, brown rice syrup, garlic, and salt in a small jar.

**Combine** the cooked eggplant and potato mixture, steamed green beans, and tofu cubes in a large salad bowl. Pour the Dijon vinaigrette over the top, and mix together. Serve warm or chill overnight to allow flavors to mingle, and serve at room temperature. You can also put some of this mixture between 2 pieces of whole grain bread for a Mediterranean grilled vegetable sandwich.

Per serving: Calories: 239, Protein: 7 gm., Fat: 10 gm., Carbohydrates: 29 gm.

# Tofu Greek Salad

Serves 6 to 8

**Prepare a marinade** by combining in a small mixing bowl the oil, water, vinegar, oregano, and thyme.

**Stir the tofu cubes** into the marinade, and let set in the refrigerator for at least one hour. The longer the tofu marinates, the more flavorful it will become.

**Add** the tomatoes, cucumber, and olives at least half an hour before serving. Serve chilled or at room temperature.

Per serving: Calories: 157, Protein: 5 gm., Fat: 13 gm., Carbohydrates: 5 gm.

¼ cup extra-virgin olive oil

¼ cup water

¼ cup wine vinegar

½ teaspoon oregano

¼ teaspoon thyme

1 pound extra-firm tofu, cut in 1-inch cubes

3 ripe, medium tomatoes, chopped

1 seedless cucumber, chopped

1 cup pitted, whole black olive

## Food for Thought . . .

You've heard the expression, "cool as a cucumber." That's because they are high in sodium and are a great summer food to help cool down the body.

# Italian Toasted Panzanella Salad

Serves 4 to 6

1 (12-inch) whole wheat
  baguette

1 teaspoon olive oil

2 tablespoons balsamic vinegar

2 tablespoons fresh basil,
  chopped

1 tablespoon olive oil

1 tablespoon water

1 head Boston or bibb lettuce,
  washed and torn in bite-size
  pieces

3 large ripe tomatoes, chopped

¼ cup red onion, minced

**Preheat** the oven to 300°.

**Cut** the baguette in half lengthwise, and sprinkle the cut sides of the baguette with 1 teaspoon oil. Cut the bread into 1-inch cubes, place on a baking sheet, and bake for 20 minutes.

**Combine** the vinegar, basil, 1 tablespoon olive oil, and water in a small jar.

**Mix** the lettuce, tomatoes, onion, and the baked baguette cubes in a medium bowl.

**Pour the dressing** over the salad ingredients, and mix well. Eat immediately or the bread will become soft.

Per serving: Calories: 166, Protein: 5 gm., Fat: 5 gm., Carbohydrates: 23 gm.

*Did you know?*

Here are the names of some famous vegetarians; Plato, William Shakespeare, Benjamin Franklin, Dr. Spock, and Linda and Paul McCartney.

# Dill Potato Salad

Serves 6

**Scrub, peel, cube, and** steam the potatoes for 15 to 20 minutes until tender.

**To make the dressing**, combine the mayonnaise, mustard, and vinegars in a blender or small bowl, using a wire whisk to blend.

**Mix** the potatoes, celery, parsley, and scallions in a large mixing bowl.

**Add** the dill and dressing, and chill for 15 minutes or longer to allow flavors to absorb into the potatoes.

Per serving: Calories: 131, Protein: 1 gm., Fat: 2 gm., Carbohydrates: 25 gm.

**Variation:** For those who do not wish to use two different vinegars, you can use one, or substitute with apple cider vinegar.

1½ pounds red potatoes

¼ cup tofu mayonnaise

1 tablespoon Dijon mustard

1 tablespoon brown rice vinegar

1 tablespoon umeboshi vinegar

1 cup celery, chopped

½ cup fresh parsley, chopped

½ cup scallions or minced red onions, chopped

2 tablespoons fresh dill, minced

## Did you know?

Parsley is rich in vitamins and minerals that are easily absorbed. It is one of the best sources of Vitamin A. Parsley has seven times the vitamin A of carrots and four times that of spinach. It is also a very important part of a reducing diet and works as a natural diuretic.

# Beet and Asparagus Salad

Serves 6

1 pound (approximately 4
   large) beets

2 pounds asparagus

2 tablespoons red onion, diced

3 tablespoons balsamic vinegar

2 tablespoons water

2 tablespoons extra-virgin
olive oil

pinch of sea salt

**Preheat** the oven to 375°.

**Wash and cut** the tops off the beets. If the beets come with the greens, save them to steam later. Place ½ cup water in a small baking dish, add the whole beets, cover with foil, and bake approximately 1 hour until tender. Set aside to cool.

**Cut off the skin**, when the beets have cooled, and cut into eighths.

**Wash and break off** the tough ends of the asparagus. Peel the lower portion of the asparagus with a vegetable peeler. Place all of the asparagus in a steamer in a medium pot, and steam for 5 to 7 minutes until tender. Rinse under cold water, drain, and set aside.

**Mix together** the red onion, vinegar, water, oil, and salt for the dressing.

**Pour** half the dressing over the beets and the other half over the asparagus. Chill for at least thirty minutes (the longer, the better).

**To serve**, spread the asparagus on a serving platter, and lay the beets around the edge. Pour the rest of the dressing over the vegetables, and serve.

Per serving: Calories: 103, Protein: 3 gm., Fat: 5 gm.,
   Carbohydrates: 12 gm.

## Food for Thought. . .

Eat to live, not live to eat.

—Benjamin Franklin

# Tricolor Bow Tie Salad with Sesame Dressing

Serves 6

**Cook** the pasta according to package directions.

**Place** the beets in a small saucepan, with enough water to cover, and cook at a low boil for about 15 minutes until tender. Drain and reserve the cooking liquid to drink or use in a soup broth. Set the beets aside.

**Steam the broccoli** for about 8 minutes until crisp-tender.

**Gently toss** the bow ties and broccoli together, and add the red pepper.

**Prepare the sesame** dressing by mixing together the oil, water, sesame seeds, tamari, mirin, and gingerroot in a jar. Shake well.

**Add the dressing** to the salad to taste, reserving any extra for other pasta or grain salads.

**Let the salad** set in the refrigerator at least half an hour. Top with the chopped beets, and serve with a cold sweet potato on the side and steamed greens. You can use the beet greens if you used fresh beets.

1 (8 oz.) package vegetable bow tie pasta

1 cup beets, peeled and cubed, or 1 small can beets

1 cup broccoli flowers, chopped

1 cup red pepper, chopped

2 tablespoons sesame oil

2 tablespoons water

1 tablespoon toasted sesame seeds

2 tablespoons tamari

1 tablespoon mirin

½ teaspoon fresh gingerroot, grated

Per serving: Calories: 179, Protein: 7 gm., Fat: 7 gm., Carbohydrates: 23 gm.

## Did you know?

The center for Science in the Public Interest found the most nutritious vegetables to be, sweet potatoes and raw carrots. Close behind were collard greens, red peppers, kale, dandelions greens, spinach, and broccoli

# Tomato Salad

Serves 3 to 4

1 pound roma tomatoes

2 cloves garlic, minced

2 tablespoons oregano

3-5 fresh basil leaves, cut into
    pieces

1 teaspoon olive oil

2 tablespoons balsamic vinegar

soy mozzarella cubes or
    marinated tofu cubes (see
    Tofu Greek Salad page 45)
    (optional)

**Chop** the roma tomatoes into bite size pieces

**Add** the remaining ingredients in a large mixing bowl.

**Place** in a food storage container, and marinate in the refrigerator for at least 30 minutes.

Per serving: Calories: 67, Protein: 2 gm., Fat: 1 gm., Carbohydrates: 11 gm.

## Did you know?

The National Academy of Science has found that certain foods offer protection against cancer: oranges, grapefruits, dark green leafy vegetables, carrots, winter squash, and tomatoes. All are rich in Vitamin C and beta carotene, the material our bodies convert to Vitamin A. (Nutrition Action Newsletter, CSPI, p. 4 July/August 1982)

# Black Olive and Tempeh Pasta Salad

Serves 6

**Steam** the tempeh for 20 minutes, cool, and cut into 1 x 1-inch pieces.

**For the marinade**, combine the tamari, lemon juice, water, mirin, and 2 cloves garlic in a small bowl.

**Add the tempeh pieces** and mix well. Refrigerate and marinate at least 30 minutes.

**Cook the rotini** according to the package directions.

**While pasta is cooking**, prepare the dressing by combining the water, vinegar, lemon juice, oil, 2 cloves garlic, and oregano in a small jar.

**Drain the cooked pasta**, cool under cold running water, and place in a large salad bowl.

**Add** the tomatoes, onion, celery, and olives. Toss the pasta and vegetables gently, add the dressing, and mix again gently. Refrigerate at least one hour until ready to serve.

**Just before serving**, heat a medium skillet, and spray it with canola mist. Add the marinated tempeh and brown lightly for about 5 to 10 minutes. Add to the other salad ingredients, toss gently, and serve, or refrigerate and eat cold.

Per serving: Calories: 224, Protein: 9 gm., Fat: 9 gm., Carbohydrates: 25 gm.

½ pound tempeh (three or five-grain tempeh if available)

2 tablespoons tamari

1 tablespoon fresh lemon juice

1 tablespoon water

1 tablespoon mirin

2 cloves garlic, minced

8-10 oz. Jerusalem artichoke pasta rotini or other rotini

½ cup water

3 tablespoons red wine vinegar

2 tablespoons fresh lemon juice

2 tablespoons olive oil

2 cloves garlic, minced

½ teaspoon oregano

3 ripe medium tomatoes, cut in 4 wedges each

½ medium onion, thinly sliced and separated into rings

2 stalks celery, thinly sliced on the diagonal

½ cup medium black olives, cut in half

*Did you know?*
_____

Pasta is great for long lasting energy.

# Three Bean Salad

1 (15 oz.) can garbanzo beans (chick-peas)

1 (15 oz.) can kidney beans

1 (15 oz.) can Great Northern or white beans

¼ pound snap beans, cut in halves

¼ cup red wine vinegar

2½ tablespoons olive oil

2½ tablespoons water

1½ tablespoons fresh lemon juice

1 tablespoon mirin

5 scallions, minced

2 cloves garlic, chopped

**Drain,** rinse, and place the canned beans in a large salad bowl.

**Steam the snap beans** for about 4 minutes until crisp-tender, add to the drained beans, and mix.

**To make the dressing,** Combine the vinegar, oil, water, lemon juice, mirin, scallions, and garlic in a small jar.

**Pour** the dressing over the beans, and mix well. Refrigerate at least 1 hour before serving, stirring the dressing into the beans several times.

Per serving: Calories: 351, Protein: 16 gm., Fat: 6 gm., Carbohydrates: 54 gm.

## Did you know?

Lemons are an excellent source of Vitamin C and help remove toxins from the body. Start the day with a cup of hot water with freshly squeezed lemon juice and some cayenne, if you like. This is a good cleanser for the liver. Drink it before anything else.

# Southwestern Black Bean Salad

Serves 8

**Mix** the beans, peppers, tomato, corn, jicama, onions, and cilantro in a large salad bowl.

**To make the dressing**, combine the oil, water, lime juice, mirin, tamari, balsamic vinegar, maple syrup, cayenne, and cumin in a small jar.

**Pour the dressing** over the salad ingredients, and mix well. Serve chilled or at room temperature.

Per serving: Calories: 234, Protein: 8 gm., Fat: 9 gm., Carbohydrates: 31 gm.

**Variation:** Replace 1 can of black beans with 1 can of pinto beans.

### About this recipe——

This salad is also delicious served on warm corn tortillas or stuffed into taco shells.

### Did you know?

Black beans are beneficial to the reproductive system and the kidneys. Black bean juice is recommended for helping to control the hot flashes associated with menopause.

2 (15 oz.) cans black beans, drained, or 4 cups cooked beans

¾ cup green pepper, diced

½ cup red pepper, diced

1 cup tomato, diced

1 cup cooked corn

½ cup jicama, diced (optional)

¼ cup red onions, diced

¼ cup fresh cilantro, minced

2 tablespoons canola oil

2 tablespoons water

2 tablespoons fresh lime juice

1 tablespoon mirin or white wine vinegar

1 tablespoon tamari

2 teaspoons balsamic vinegar

1½ teaspoons maple syrup

⅛ teaspoon cayenne

1 teaspoon cumin

# Garlic Herb Dressing

Yield: 1 cup

¼ cup flax oil

¼ cup olive oil

¼ cup + 1 tablespoon low-
sodium soy sauce

3 tablespoons red wine vinegar

1 tablespoon mirin

¼ cup fruit-sweetened ketchup

1 teaspoon fresh lemon juice

¾ teaspoon vegetarian
Worcestershire sauce

1 tablespoon crushed garlic

1 teaspoon Italian herb
seasoning

1 teaspoon maple syrup

**Blend** all the ingredients together. Keep refrigerated. For a slightly spicier flavor, add a dash or two of hot sauce. Serve on salads, spinach salad, steamed vegetables such as broccoli and greens, and use as a dressing on raw veggies stuffed in pita pockets. For a thinner dressing, add more mirin.

Per tablespoon: Calories: 70, Protein: 1 gm., Fat: 6 gm., Carbohydrates: 2 gm.

## Did you know?

Mirin is a rice wine which can be substituted for white wine.

# Basic Miso Dressing

Yield: about ¾ cup

**Combine** all of the ingredients in a small jar. Keep refrigerated.

Per tablespoon: Calories: 53, Protein: 0 gm.,
Fat: 4 gm., Carbohydrates: 3 gm.

¼ cup canola oil

¼ cup water

2 tablespoons brown rice syrup
or honey

2 tablespoons brown rice or
apple cider vinegar

2 tablespoons scallions, minced

1 tablespoon miso

*About this recipe*———

This dressing is delicious on tossed Romaine lettuce with sliced cucumbers and grated carrots.

*Did you know?*

Miso is a cultured food made from soybeans. Unpasteurized miso is rich in lactic acid forming bacteria and enzymes which aid digestion.

# Rice and Vegetable Soup

Serves 6 to 8

½ cup organic, short grain
    brown rice

6 cups water

1 medium onion, chopped

3 carrots, chopped in chunks

1 potato, peeled and chopped

1 parsnip, peeled and chopped

¼ cup mild miso

½ cup water

**Clean and rinse** the rice, and place in a soup pot with 6 cups water.

**Add** the onion, carrots, potato, and parsnip, bring to a boil, then lower the heat to medium. Cover and cook about 30 minutes until the vegetables are tender. Remove from the heat.

**Use a wire whisk** to dissolve the miso and ½ cup water in a small mixing bowl.

**Add** the miso broth to the soup pot, let set another 5 to 10 minutes, then serve warm. It is important to never boil miso, or the healthy enzymes in the miso that are so beneficial to the digestive tract will be destroyed.

Per serving: Calories: 123, Protein: 3 gm., Fat: 0 gm., Carbohydrates: 26 gm.

## Did you know?

Fat contains nine calories per gram. Protein and carbohydrates contain only four calories per gram.

# Minestrone Soup

Serves 8 to 10

**Sauté** the garlic, onion, carrots, and celery in the oil for about 5 minutes in a large soup pot on medium-high heat.

**Add** the bay leaves, basil, thyme, and black pepper to the soup pot, and cook 5 more minutes.

**Mix** ½ cup water and the vegetable broth powder, and add to the soup pot.

**Add** the tomatoes, beans, cabbage, macaroni, and 6 cups water, and let simmer until the vegetables are tender, about 25 minutes.

**Add the green beans** toward the end of cooking, and cook until tender.

**Flavor the soup**, by adding the vinegar, tamari, and salt. If the soup is too thick, thin it with more water. Serve with hot bread.

Per serving: Calories: 115, Protein: 5 gm., Fat: 0 gm., Carbohydrates: 21 gm.

*Did you know?*

Beans give us a lot of good energy and staying power which is great for a physical laborer. They are high in potassium and phosphorus.

2 large cloves garlic, minced

1 large onion, chopped

2 carrots, chopped

2 celery stalks, chopped

1 teaspoon olive oil

2 bay leaves

2 tablespoons dried basil

1 teaspoon thyme

¼ teaspoon black pepper

½ cup water

1 teaspoon vegetable broth powder

2½ cups canned whole tomatoes, chopped with juice

1 cup cooked garbanzo beans (chick-peas)

1 cup cooked cannelini beans (white kidney beans)

½ small head green cabbage, chopped

½ cup uncooked elbow macaroni

6 cups water

1 cup fresh green beans, cut in 1-inch lengths

2 tablespoons balsamic vinegar

1 tablespoon tamari

½ teaspoon sea salt

# Mushroom Barley Soup

Serves 6

1 teaspoon olive oil or oil spray

2 carrots, diced

1 onion, chopped

2 stalks celery, diced

2 cups fresh white mushrooms,
   stems trimmed and thinly
   sliced

2 tablespoons tamari

1 teaspoon each: dry basil,
   thyme, and oregano

½ -1 teaspoon sea salt

7 cups vegetable stock or water

½ cup hulled or pearl barley

3 tablespoons fresh parsley,
   minced

**Heat a large soup pot,** add the oil, and sauté the carrots, onion, and celery over medium heat about 5 minutes until slightly softened.

**Add** the mushrooms and raise the heat to medium-high to allow the mushrooms to "sweat," about 5 minutes, stirring often.

**Add** the tamari, spices, salt, and vegetable stock, bring to a boil, and simmer for 5 minutes to combine flavors.

**Rinse the barley** until the water runs clear. You can also roast the barley in a dry skillet until it exudes a nutty aroma.

**Add the barley** to the soup, and simmer, stirring occasionally, until the barley is tender, about 45 minutes.

**Stir in the parsley,** adjust the seasonings, and serve.

Per serving: Calories: 64, Protein: 2 gm., Fat: 1 gm., Carbohydrates: 12 gm.

**Variation:** For an extra boost of calcium, add 1 cup chopped kale during the last 5 minutes of simmering.

**Variation:** Substitute shiitake mushrooms for a portion of the 2 cups of mushrooms. They stimulate the immune system to produce more interferon which fights viruses and cancer. Shiitake also contain Vitamin D which is needed for the absorption of calcium.

## Did you know?

If you want to add more fiber to your diet, keep cooked barley in the refrigerator (up to one week) or in the freezer (one to two months), and stir ¼ to ½ cup into salads, soups, and pasta sauce.

## Did you know?

A half cup of cooked barley provides 13 gm. of protein. Hulled barley has a superior nutrient content and is richer in dietary fiber than pearled barley, because only the outer, inedible hull, not the bran, is removed.

# Grannie's Vegetable Soup

Serves 12

**Soak** the lima beans overnight in water, drain, and rinse.

**Combine** the lima beans, water, onions, celery, carrots, and tomatoes, in a large soup pot. Cover the pot with a lid. Bring to a boil, reduce the heat to medium-high, and simmer for about 45 minutes.

**Add** the corn, lima beans, peas, bay leaves, garlic powder, peppercorns, parsley, and broth mixture to the soup pot.

**Continue cooking** 30 more minutes until the beans are tender. If the soup is too thick, add more broth mixture. If you prefer a spicier soup, you can add pepper and other spices.

Per serving: Calories: 158, Protein: 8 gm., Fat: 0 gm., Carbohydrates: 31 gm.

1 cup dried lima beans

14 cups water

2 medium onions, chopped

3 stalks celery, chopped

3 carrots, chopped

1 (28 oz.) can chopped tomatoes

2 cups frozen yellow corn

1 (16 oz.) package frozen lima beans

2 cups frozen peas

2 bay leaves

2 teaspoons garlic powder

7 peppercorns

3 tablespoons parsley, chopped

1 cup water mixed with 2 tablespoons vegetable broth powder

## About this recipe——

This recipe makes a large pot of soup. Freeze some and save for future lunches.

## About this recipe——

Here's a quick-soak method if you forget or don't want to soak the beans overnight. Place the beans and enough water to cover in a pot. Cover the pot, bring to a boil, turn off the heat, and let set one hour. Drain and use the same as beans soaked overnight.

# Creamy Potato Soup

Serves 8

4 cups water

1 tablespoon dried vegetable
  broth powder, or
  1 vegetable bouillon cube

2 cups onions, chopped

3 medium potatoes, peeled
  and cubed

⅛ teaspoon cayenne

pinch of sea salt

¼ cup plain soymilk

⅓ cup soy sour cream

¼ cup soy cheddar cheese,
  grated

**Mix together**, in a large soup pot, the water, vegetable broth, onions, potatoes, cayenne, and salt. Bring to a boil, lower the heat, cover, and simmer for 25 minutes until the potatoes are tender.

**Remove half of the potato mixture**, and process in a blender or food processor until well blended. Pour the pureed mixture back into the soup, add the soymilk, and cook over medium heat until well heated.

**Stir in** the soy sour cream and cheese, and cook 1 more minute.

**Ladle the soup** into serving bowls, and garnish with chopped parsley if desired.

Per serving: Calories: 83, Protein: 2 gm., Fat: 2 gm., Carbohydrates: 14 gm.

## Did you know?

Kale is as good a source of calcium as milk. Five ounces of raw kale, or a half cup cooked, has as much calcium (300 mg) as an 8 oz. glass of milk. (Health, July 1, Aug. 1990)

Beautiful Beans and
Great Grains

# Lentil & Seitan Sausage Stew

Serves 10

1 pound dry lentils

5 cups water

½ teaspoon sea salt

½ teaspoon dry, hot mustard

½ teaspoon ginger powder

¼ teaspoon cinnamon

2 cups tomato juice

2 cups tomato sauce

3 tablespoons maple syrup

3 tablespoons barbecue sauce

1 large onion, chopped

16 oz. sausage seitan, cut in chunks

**Place the lentils** in a large pot with the water, spices, tomato juice, tomato sauce, maple syrup, and barbecue sauce. Bring to a boil, lower the heat to a simmer, cover, and cook for about 45 minutes.

**Sauté** the onion and sausage seitan in a nonstick skillet lightly sprayed with olive oil, and brown for a few minutes. You may need to add 1 to 2 tablespoons of water if it begins to stick to the pan.

**Add the browned seitan** to the pot, and simmer for 15 more minutes.

Per serving: Calories: 178, Protein: 20 gm., Fat: 0 gm., Carbohydrates: 23 gm.

# Chick-peas and Spinach

Serves 4

1 (10 oz.) package fresh spinach, chopped

1 (15 oz.) can garbanzo beans (chick-peas), rinsed and drained

2 cloves garlic, minced

¼ cup red onion, chopped

juice of 1 lemon

1 teaspoon tamari

pinch of sea salt

**Wash and drain** the spinach, and steam for 3 to 4 minutes.

**Gently mix** all of the ingredients together in a medium-size mixing bowl.

Per serving: Calories: 198, Protein: 10 gm., Fat: 2 gm., Carbohydrates: 33 gm.

# Black Bean Chili

Serves 4

**Sauté,** in a large soup pot, the onions, garlic, carrots, and peppers in the orange juice. Add the cumin and cook on medium heat for about 4 minutes.

**Add** the black beans, green chilies, vegetable broth mix, tomatoes, and maple syrup.

**Cook** on medium-high heat for about 25 minutes until the chili thickens.

**Garnish** with chopped cilantro and a dollop of soy sour cream or grated soy Monterey Jack cheese. For a spicier chili, add 1 to 2 teaspoons chili powder. To make this a heartier meal, serve over brown rice.

Per serving: Calories: 299, Protein: 15 gm., Fat: 1 gm., Carbohydrates: 58 gm.

### Did you know?

Beans are an excellent source of fiber. They have more soluble fiber than oats. One cup of beans a day is as effective at lowering cholesterol as ⅔ cup of oat bran. Beans are also a good source of folic acid, a B vitamin which is important for building protein and red blood cells.

1½ cups onions, chopped

2 large cloves garlic, minced

½ cup carrots, chopped

½ cup yellow or green peppers, chopped

½ cup orange juice

2 teaspoons cumin

4 cups canned black beans, rinsed and drained

½ cup mild green chilies

2 cups water mixed with 2 teaspoons dried vegetable broth

1 (15 oz.) can crushed tomatoes

2 teaspoons maple syrup

cilantro

soy sour cream (optional)

soy Monterey Jack cheese (optional)

1-2 teaspoons chili powder (optional)

# Aunt Linda's Baked Beans

Serves 8

1½ green peppers, chopped

2 large yellow onions, chopped

2-3 teaspoons water or olive oil

2 (4½ oz.) jars of mushrooms

2 (16 oz.) cans vegetarian
  baked beans

⅓ - ⅔ cup Dijon mustard

¾ cup barbecue sauce

pinch of black pepper

**Preheat** the oven to 350°.

**Sauté**, in a large skillet, the green peppers, and onions in the water.

**Add** the mushrooms, baked beans, mustard, barbecue sauce, and black pepper, and mix well.

**Pour** into a casserole dish, and bake for 1 hour.

Per serving: Calories: 188, Protein: 6 gm., Fat: 3 gm.,
  Carbohydrates: 33 gm.

**Variation:** Add 5 tablespoons textured vegetable protein soaked in 5 tablespoons warm water.

Per serving: Calories: 198, Protein: 8 gm., Fat: 3 gm.,
  Carbohydrates: 34 gm.

## Did you know?

When asked what one bit of advice he would give people hoping to prevent coronary disease and increase longevity, William Castelli, M.D., director of the Framingham Heart Study, said, "Go on a vegetarian diet."

# Salsa Rice

Serves 6

**Cook** the rice according to package directions.

**Add** the salsa and mix in with the rice

**Garnish** each serving with the green onions.

Per serving: Calories: 76, Protein: 3 gm., Fat: 0 gm.,
Carbohydrates: 16 gm.

1 box quick cooking Spanish
flavor brown rice pilaf

1 (8-10 oz.) jar mild salsa
(unless you like hot!)

½ cup green onions with
greens, chopped

## Did you know?

Here is a warning from the Center for Science in the Public Interest, in their April 1988, Nutrition Action Newsletter. "Be sure to eat less fat in the second decade of life—from the teen years on. Studies indicate that the seeds of breast cancer are sown during puberty. Whether those seeds grow into cancer may depend, on part, on what a woman eats from puberty on." Dr. Leonard Cohen says, "Since the initiating action occurs at puberty, the sooner women eat a low-fat diet and exercise, the better."

# Sushi Rice

Serves 2 to 3

⅓ cup sweet rice

⅔ cup short-grain brown rice

1½-2 cups water

1 teaspoon brown rice vinegar

1 teaspoon mirin, brown rice
    syrup, or maple syrup

**Wash** the rice well, drain, and place in a medium-size pot.

**Add** the water and a pinch of sea salt, cover, and bring to a boil.

**Prepare** another burner (if your stovetop is electric) on medium-low heat using a flame deflector (available in hardware stores and some kitchen stores).

**When the rice comes to a boil**, transfer the pot to the prepared burner, and cook for 40 minutes.

**Remove** the pot from the heat, sprinkle with the vinegar and mirin, and mix gently. Cover and set aside.

Per serving: Calories: 167, Protein: 3 gm., Fat: 0 gm.,
    Carbohydrates: 36 gm.

# Sushi

Serves 3 to 4

2 sheets nori seaweed

bamboo sushi mat

2 cups cooked Sushi Rice

2 carrots, cut into thin match
    sticks

4 scallion greens, chopped

2 teaspoons umeboshi paste

bowl of water

**Place** the nori sheet, shiny side down, on a bamboo mat.

**Place** 1 cup rice in the center of the mat, and spread evenly over the nori, leaving a top margin of 1 inch, and bottom margin of ¼ inch. Dip your hands in water from time to time to prevent the rice from sticking.

**Steam** the carrots for about 3 minutes, and let cool.

**Cut** the scallion greens into 8-inch lengths.

**Spread** the umeboshi paste over the rice in a horizontal line on the end nearest you. Lay the carrot strips on top of the paste and the scallions on top of the carrots.

**Roll up** fairly tight, pressing with the sushi mat while rolling, but trying not to touch the rice with your fingers or the mat.

**Moisten** the top edge of the nori with water, and press to seal. Place the sushi on a cutting board, seam side down. Wet a very sharp knife with hot water, and slice the sushi in half. Remoisten the knife after each slice. Cut each half in half again and each fourth in half. One sushi roll yields 6 large, 8 medium, or 10 small slices.

**Store** the sushi slices in a covered container in the refrigerator. The slices will keep for several days since the umeboshi paste acts as a preservative.

Per serving: Calories: 67, Protein: 1 gm., Fat: 0 gm., Carbohydrates: 15 gm.

# Sushi Filling Ideas

**Spread** wasabi alternately with umeboshi paste in parallel lines along the bottom edge of the rice.

**Make** a California Roll with sliced avocado, or sprinkle the rice with black sesame seeds. Cooked beans can be added for a complete protein roll.

**Variation:** Make rice balls by cutting 1 sheet of nori into fourths. Form the rice into a solidly formed ball or triangle. Press to make a hole in center of the rice. Insert some umeboshi paste into the hole or half of an actual umeboshi plum, and cover with the rice. Place ¼ of the nori on the rice ball, dampen your hands, and place another ¼ nori on the rice ball. Moisten the edge of the nori with water, and press to seal. These rice balls are great for traveling, lunch boxes, or snacking.

pickled ginger

thinly sliced cucumbers cut lengthwise

wasabi (Japanese horseradish paste)

# Little Jack Horner Cones
## (for kids)

**Take** a quarter sheet of the nori, and roll up into a cone shape. Scoop some rice into the cone. Let your child stick in their thumb and push in an umeboshi plum. You can also include fresh carrots and cucumbers.

# Dipping Sauces for Sushi

1. **Mix** equal parts tamari, water, and lemon juice.
2. **The same as number 1**, but add freshly minced ginger and garlic.
3. **Mix** equal parts tamari, water, and mirin.
4. **Mix** 1 tablespoon wasabi powder with 1 teaspoon water.

# Baked Rice

Serves 4

**Preheat** the oven to 350°.

**In a medium-size mixing bowl**, mix the rice, broth, onion, lemon juice, and lemon peel.

**Pour** into a casserole dish, and bake for 45 minutes. Serve warm.

Per serving: Calories: 120, Protein: 3 gm., Fat: 0 gm., Carbohydrates: 26 gm.

1 cup long grain brown rice

2 cups vegetable or mock chicken broth

4 tablespoons onion, chopped

2 tablespoons lemon juice

½ teaspoon grated lemon peel

## Did you know?

Brown rice contains twice as much fiber as white rice.

# Indian Rice

Yield: 4¼ cups (serves 4)

**Lightly spray** a medium-size saucepan with cooking oil, and sauté the cumin and bay leaves for about 3 to 4 minutes.

**Add** the basmati rice and sauté 2 more minutes.

**Add** the water, bring to a boil, and cover. Lower the heat and simmer for about 30 minutes until done.

Per serving: Calories: 230, Protein: 5 gm., Fat: 0 gm., Carbohydrates: 50 gm.

½ teaspoon cumin seeds

2 bay leaves

1 cup basmati rice

2 cups water

## About this recipe

This is great with Vegetable Stir Fry (page 120).

# Kashi Salad

## Serves 8 to 10

1 cup kashi

2 cups water

½ red pepper, chopped

½ cup red onion, chopped

¼ cup almonds, chopped

¼ cup canola oil

¼ cup water

2 tablespoons tamari

3 tablespoons red wine vinegar

**In a medium-size pot**, mix the kashi and water, and simmer on medium-high heat for about 35 to 40 minutes until cooked through. Set aside to cool.

**While the kashi is cooking**, mix the red pepper, red onion, and almonds in a medium-size mixing bowl.

**Add** the kashi and mix well.

**To make the dressing**, combine the oil, water, tamari, and vinegar in a small bowl.

**Pour** the dressing over the kashi and vegetables, and mix. Cover and chill before serving. Garnish with romaine or bib lettuce.

Per serving: Calories: 139, Protein: 2 gm., Fat: 8 gm., Carbohydrates: 13 gm.

## Did you know?

Whole grains contain complex carbohydrates and are a great way to get fiber in your diet.

# Oil-Free Sweet Bulgur Salad

Serves 6

**Dry roast** the bulgur in a small skillet on medium heat for 5 minutes until a nutty aroma is emitted, stirring occasionally.

**Rinse** the bulgur and drain.

**Place** the bulgur in a medium-size bowl, and cover with 1 cup boiling water. Let set approximately 1 hour until the liquid is absorbed. Squeeze dry the bulgur.

**Add** the parsley, mint, red pepper, and scallions, and mix.

**To make the dressing,** combine the lemon juice, orange juice, tamari, salt, cumin, and basil in a small bowl.

**Pour** the dressing over the bulgur and vegetables, and mix together. Refrigerate until served.

1 cup bulgur

1 cup boiling water

1 cup packed Italian flat parsley, chopped

1 cup fresh mint, minced

½ cup red pepper, chopped

4 scallions, chopped

¼ cup lemon juice

½ cup orange juice

2 tablespoons tamari

½ teaspoon sea salt

1 teaspoon cumin

1 teaspoon basil

Per serving: Calories: 116, Protein: 4 gm., Fat: 0 gm., Carbohydrates: 24 gm.

## About this recipe——

This is a variation on the traditional Middle Eastern tabouli salad which typically contains a lot of parsley and only a small amount of bulgur. Americans tend to like their tabouli with a lot more bulgur.

## Did you know?

Here's a tip for chopping the parsley and mint. Place them in the freezer for 1 to 2 hours to flash freeze until they are semi-firm. Then process in a food processor. After the mint and parsley are all chopped up, rinse under hot water to bring out the flavor.

# Oriental Rice Salad with Tamari Orange Dressing

Serves 6

2 cups cooked long grain
   brown rice

¼ cup slivered almonds, roasted

½ cup red or yellow bell
   peppers, chopped

½ cup celery, chopped

½ cup snow peas, diagonally
   sliced

¼ cup raisins, soaked and
   drained

2 scallions, chopped

¼ cup + 2 tablespoons fresh
   orange juice

¼ cup water, or 2 tablespoons
   water + 2 tablespoons canola
   or flax oil

2 tablespoons lemon juice

2 tablespoons soy sauce

2 tablespoons mirin

½ teaspoon fresh gingerroot,
   minced

2 cloves garlic, minced

**In a large mixing bowl**, mix the rice, almonds, peppers, celery, snow peas, raisins, and scallions.

**To prepare the dressing**, prepare the dressing combine the orange juice, oil, lemon juice, soy sauce, mirin, gingerroot, and garlic in a small bowl.

**Pour** the dressing over the salad ingredients. Chill for at least 1 hour before serving (the longer, the better). Garnish the salad with bibb lettuce.

Per serving: Calories: 154, Protein: 4 gm., Fat: 3 gm.,
   Carbohydrates: 27 gm.

## Did you know?

Limonene, found in lemons and orange rinds, stimulates the production of enzymes that may help dispose of potential carcinogens.

# Eric's Lentil Barley Salad

Serves 4 to 6

**Soak** the the barley in water overnight, drain, and rinse.

**In a medium saucepan**, boil the soaked barley in ¾ cup water for 1 hour. Drain, rinse in cold water until completely cooled, and drain well again.

**Rinse** the lentils. In a medium saucepan, bring the lentils and 2¼ cups water to a boil. Reduce the heat, cover, and simmer for 15 minutes. Do not let the lentils go above a simmer or they will split.

**Drain** the lentils, rinse in cold water, and drain well again.

**Combine** the barley, lentils, zucchini, squash, carrots, walnuts, and canola oil.

**To make the dressing**, combine the vinegar, basil, dill, oil, lemon juice, brown rice syrup, horseradish, garlic, salt, and black pepper, and mix well.

**Pour** the dressing over the barley salad, and gently fold together to combine. Refrigerate for several hours to let the flavors blend. Serve chilled or at room temperature. This will keep, refrigerated, for 3 to 5 days.

Per serving: Calories: 213, Protein: 6 gm., Fat: 9 gm., Carbohydrates: 25 gm.

**Variation:** To give this salad an Italian flavor, substitute red wine vinegar for the lemon juice, reduce the brown rice vinegar to 4 teaspoons, omit the brown rice syrup, and add 4 teaspoons balsamic vinegar. This makes a slightly more robust salad. You can also increase the fresh basil to ⅓ cup, and omit the fresh dill for more Italian flavor.

¼ cup hulled or pearled barley

¾ cup water

¾ cup dry lentils

2¼ cups water

¼ cup zucchini, diced

¼ cup yellow squash, diced

¼ cup carrots, chopped

¼ cup walnuts, toasted and coarsely chopped

1 tablespoon canola oil

3 tablespoons + 1 teaspoon brown rice or apple cider vinegar

3 tablespoons fresh basil, chopped

2-3 tablespoons fresh dill, chopped, or 2 teaspoons dill weed

1-1½ tablespoons extra-virgin olive oil

2 teaspoons fresh lemon juice

2 teaspoons brown rice syrup or honey

1 teaspoon prepared horseradish, or to taste

1 clove garlic, minced

¼ teaspoon sea salt

¼ teaspoon black pepper

# Cornmeal Biscuits

Makes 8 medium biscuits

1⅓ cups white wheat flour

½ cup cornmeal

2½ teaspoons baking powder

½ cup fat-free soy cheddar
    cheese

½ teaspoon sea salt

1 teaspoon dry mustard

¼ cup + 2 teaspoons
    applesauce

⅔ cup low-fat rice or soymilk

**Preheat** the oven to 375°.

**Mix** the flour, cornmeal, baking powder, soy cheese, sea salt, and dry mustard.

**Add** the applesauce and blend with a fork until the mixture resembles a coarse meal.

**Add** the rice or soymilk, and form into dough. Place the dough on a floured cutting board, and knead for about 6 to 7 minutes.

**Spread** out ½ inch thick, and cut with a biscuit cutter.

**Bake** on a lightly oiled cookie sheet for 15 minutes until browned.

Per biscuit: Calories: 138, Protein: 5 gm., Fat: 3 gm.,
    Carbohydrates: 23 gm.

## Did you know?

If you want to add more fiber to your diet, keep cooked barley in the refrigerator (up to one week) or in the freezer (one to two months), and stir ¼ to ½ cup into salads, soups, and pasta sauce.

Mexican Olé Cuisine

# Taco Olé Salad

Serves 4 to 6

1 (15 oz.) can kidney beans, rinsed and drained

2 tomatoes, chopped

1 head Romaine lettuce, cleaned and broken into pieces

1 medium onion, chopped

¼ cup black olives, chopped

1 cup hot or mild salsa

¼ cup Thousand Island dressing

6 oz. corn tortilla chips (regular or baked), crumbled in large pieces

**In a large salad bowl**, combine the kidney beans, tomatoes, lettuce, onion, olives, and salsa.

**Just before serving**, add the dressing and tortilla chips. If desired, you can add more dressing to the salad. If your packing your lunch, keep the chips separate until just before eating.

Per serving: Calories: 346, Protein: 10 gm., Fat: 11 gm., Carbohydrates: 53 gm.

# Oven Roasted Red Peppers

Yield: 2 roasted peppers

2 red peppers

*About this recipe——*

This a good, basic recipe that you can use to create your own delicious roasted red peppers.

**Preheat** the oven to 500°.

**Line** a baking sheet with aluminum foil, place the peppers on their sides, and bake for 20 minutes until their skins are charred.

**Using tongs**, place the hot baked peppers in a heavy-duty zip lock plastic bag, and seal. Set aside for 10 minutes to allow the peppers to steam and separate from their skins.

**Use** the tongs to remove the peppers from the bag. Peel the skins and remove the membranes and seeds from inside the peppers. Discard the charred skins and the seeds.

Per serving: Calories: 5, Protein: 0 gm., Fat: 0 gm., Carbohydrates: 1 gm.

# Vegetarian Tacos

Serves 8

**In a medium-size skillet**, sauté the onion, green pepper, and garlic in the water.

**Add** the tomato sauce, pinto beans, corn, chili powder, and cumin.

**Fill** the Taco Shells with the bean mixture, and garnish with the lettuce, tomatoes, salsa, and tofu sour cream. The bean filling can also be used in whole wheat tortillas.

Per serving: Calories: 185, Protein: 7 gm., Fat: 1 gm., Carbohydrates: 36 gm.

**Variation:** Serve Vegetarian Tacos over 1 cup cooked long grain brown rice, and garnish with salsa.

*Did you know?*

Only animal products contain cholesterol.

1 small onion, chopped

½ green pepper, chopped

2 cloves garlic. minced

2 tablespoons water

8 oz. tomato sauce

1 (15 oz.) can pinto beans, rinsed and drained

1 cup corn

2 teaspoons chili powder

1 teaspoon cumin

8 Taco Salad Shells (page 77)

2 cups lettuce, shredded

1½ cups tomatoes, chopped

1½ cups salsa

tofu sour cream (optional)

# Taco Salad Shells

Yield: 8 bowls

**Preheat** the oven to 350°.

**Tuck** the tortillas into four oven proof soup bowls or ramekins, and place in the oven. Bake for 10 minutes. Add vegetarian taco filling and garnishes.

Per tortilla (corn): Calories: 65, Protein: 2 gm., Fat: 1 gm., Carbohydrates: 12 gm.

Per tortilla (wheat): Calories: 80, Protein: 2 gm., Fat: 2 gm., Carbohydrates: 14 gm.

8 corn or wheat tortillas

# Black Bean and Red Pepper Tostadas

Serves 4

1 cup yellow summer squash, cut into rounds

1 (15 oz.) can black beans, rinsed and drained, or 1 cup instant dried black beans

1 cup Maureen's Healthy Grains (page 78)

4 corn tortillas

½ cup roasted red peppers

**Steam** the the squash in a little water until tender.

**Mash** the beans or prepare the instant beans.

**Preheat** the oven to 400°.

**Spread** ¼ cup Maureen's Healthy Grains on each tortilla, and spread ¼ cup of the beans on top of that. Lay 3 or 4 strips of roasted red pepper over each tortilla, and put 5 rounds of yellow squash around the outer edge.

**Bake** for 15 minutes. Serve with 1 or 2 tablespoons of salsa on each tortilla.

Per serving: Calories: 272, Protein: 12 gm., Fat: 1 gm., Carbohydrates: 51 gm.

# Maureen's Healthy Grains

Serves 4 to 6

1 cup basmati rice

½ cup millet

2 tablespoons quinoa

1 tablespoon amaranth

3¼ cups cold water

pinch of sea salt

**Wash** all of the grains well, and drain.

**Place** the grains, water, and salt in a medium saucepan, and bring to a boil.

**Reduce** the heat to medium, cover, and simmer for 20 to 25 minutes until all of the grains are tender.

Per serving: Calories: 196, Protein: 5 gm., Fat: 1 gm., Carbohydrates: 40 gm.

## Did you know?

Amaranth was used by the ancient Aztecs. It is high in protein and calcium. Making it especially good for children, pregnant and nursing women, and people doing heavy physical labor.

# Bean Dip Tortilla Sandwich

## Serves 4

**Steam** the broccoli until tender.

**Warm** the tortillas on a hot griddle for 10 to 15 seconds on a side, and keep warm in a tortilla server or under a clean towel until ready to use.

**Spread** each tortilla with 3 tablespoons bean dip, and top with the sprouts, and Oven Roasted Red Pepper.

**Fold up** one end of each tortilla, fold over one side, roll up, and enjoy.

Per serving: Calories: 135, Protein: 5 gm., Fat: 2 gm., Carbohydrates: 24 gm.

1 cup fresh or frozen broccoli, chopped

4 large whole wheat or corn tortillas

¾ cup vegetarian (lard-free) pinto, or 1 (9 oz.) can black bean dip

1 cup alfalfa or clover sprouts

4 slices Oven Roasted Red Peppers, (page 76)

## About this recipe——

Bean dip is a real time-saver in this recipe. Try the addition of steamed broccoli for a nutritional boost and a delicious variation on this south-of-the-border staple.

## Did you know?

Don't throw away broccoli stems; peel and eat them. They contain more fiber than the flower.

# Fifteen Minute Bean Tacos

Yield: 6 tacos

6 corn taco shells

½ (16 oz.) can vegetarian refried beans

¼ cup onions, chopped optional)

1½ cups romaine lettuce, chopped

mild salsa

Mock Guacamole (page 32) or Lime Yogurt Guacamole (page 33) (optional)

**Preheat** the oven to 350°.

**Fill** the taco shells with the refried beans.

**Put** about 1 tablespoon of onion per taco shell.

**Cook** in the oven for 15 minutes.

**Fill** each taco with ¼ cup lettuce, salsa, and guacamole, and eat warm.

Per taco: Calories: 112, Protein: 3 gm., Fat: 2 gm., Carbohydrates: 20 gm.

## About this recipe—

For brown bagging, wrap the taco in tin foil, place the lettuce in a small baggie, and put the salsa and guacamole in small containers.

## Did you know?

Soluble fiber, found in beans, oats, and oat bran, can help lower cholesterol. It can also help control hypoglycemia and diabetes by slowing down dramatic swings in blood sugar levels.

# Steamed Tortillas

**Fill** a medium-size pot with 1 inch of water, and place a steamer basket in the pot. Line the steamer with a clean kitchen towel.

**Lay** the corn or wheat tortillas on the towel and fold up the edges. Cover the pot with a lid, bring the water to a boil, and boil for about 1 minute. Remove the pot from the heat, and let set with the lid on for 15 minutes.

**Fill** the tortillas with the Broiled Vegetable Medley (page 97) or the Mock Guacamole (page 32), and serve with salsa. This is great for those having the luxury of eating at home.

corn or wheat tortillas

Per tortilla (corn): Calories: 65, Protein: 2 gm., Fat: 1 gm., Carbohydrates: 12 gm.

Per tortilla (wheat): Calories: 80, Protein: 2 gm., Fat: 2 gm., Carbohydrates: 14 gm.

# Stacked Tortillas

Serves 1

**Spread** one tortilla with ¼ cup Black Bean Chili.

**Place** another tortilla on top of the chili, repeat the bean mixture again, then add another tortilla.

**Place** ¼ cup salsa on top, garnish with cilantro, and soy cheddar cheese, and bake in a 350° oven for about 20 to 25 minutes until warmed through. Serve with a simple salad and some rice if desired. If your packing your lunch, place the tortillas in a separate container until ready to eat.

3 corn tortillas

¾ cup Black Bean Chili
   (page 63)

¼ cup salsa

cilantro

fat-free soy cheddar cheese
   (optional)

Per serving: Calories: 365, Protein: 14 gm., Fat: 3 gm., Carbohydrates: 69 gm.

*About this recipe*————

Here's a neat leftover idea using the Black Bean Chili.

# Veggie Fajitas

Yield: 4 fajita sandwiches

1 (6 oz.) package marinated
   seitan (reserve the marinade)

2 cups assorted red, yellow,
   and green peppers, chopped

½ large red onion, sliced in half
   then julienned

2 cloves of garlic, minced

¼ cup seitan marinade

2 teaspoons dried cilantro
   leaves

1 teaspoon basil

½ teaspoon garlic powder

½ teaspoon cumin

¼ teaspoon black pepper

4 whole wheat tortillas,
   warmed

**Spray** a cooking pan with olive oil, and brown the seitan on each side for 3 minutes. Cut the seitan into long thin strips, and set aside.

**Spray** a large frying pan with olive oil cooking spray, and sauté the peppers, onion, and garlic for about 10 minutes.

**Add** the seitan to the vegetables and ¼ cup marinating liquid from the seitan package.

**Add** all the herbs and spices, and simmer until the liquid is absorbed.

**Place** ¾ cup of the mixture in the middle a whole wheat tortilla, and roll up. If desired, you can sprinkle hot sauce on the mixture, and garnish with fresh cilantro leaves and soy sour cream.

Per fajita: Calories: 170, Protein: 17 gm.,
   Fat: 2 gm., Carbohydrates: 21 gm.

## Did you know?

Garlic is a great antiseptic. Its high sulphur content helps make the brain more active.

# Veritable Vegetable Dishes

# Microwave Corn in the Husk

Yield: 8 ears of corn

8 ears corn

**Place** 8 ears of corn in water to cover, and soak for about 10 minutes, leaving the corn in the husk. Drain.

**Place** the ears, 2 at a time, in the microwave, and cook for 5 minutes (cooking time is approximately 2½ minutes per ear of corn). Repeat until all 8 cobs are cooked, keeping them in the husk to keep warm until ready to eat. Peel away the husk from the kernels (the hair will come right off), and serve.

Per ear: Calories: 83, Protein: 2 gm., Fat: 0 gm., Carbohydrates: 5 gm.

**Variation:** Spread umeboshi paste lightly over the corn cobs. This is a nice, healthy replacement for butter and salt. You can presoak the corn and heat later, or cook at home and just reheat later.

# Summertime Zucchini and Red Peppers

Serves 4

2 teaspoons extra-virgin olive oil

6 zucchini, chopped

2 teaspoons tamari

juice of ¼ lemon

½ red pepper, chopped

**Place** the olive oil in a large skillet, turn the heat to medium high, add the zucchini, and cook for 5 minutes.

**Pour** the tamari and lemon juice over the zucchini. Mix well and cook 2 more minutes. Add the red pepper and cook 10 more minutes until tender.

Per serving: Calories: 47, Protein: 2 gm., Fat: 2 gm., Carbohydrates: 5 gm.

# Summer Squash with Roma Tomatoes

Serves 4

**In a large skillet**, sauté the squash and zucchini in the oil on medium-high heat for 10 minutes.

**Mix** in the tomatoes and sauté 10 more minutes.

**Sprinkle** on the herbs and cheese.

**Place** a lid on the skillet, and turn off the heat. Let set for a few minutes until the cheese melts. Serve warm. This is also good leftover cold.

Per serving: Calories: 39, Protein: 1 gm., Fat: 1 gm., Carbohydrates: 6 gm.

2 yellow squash, chopped in ½ moons

2 zucchini, chopped in ½ moons

1 teaspoon olive oil

3 roma tomatoes, chopped

1 teaspoon oregano

½ teaspoon thyme

2 to 3 tablespoons cilantro, loosely chopped

3 tablespoons soy Monterey Jack cheese, grated (optional)

*Did you know?*

Quercetin, a potent anti-carcinogen, has been recognized as a chemical with the potential to reverse the development of tumors. Large amounts of quercetin have been found in summer squash, broccoli, and particularly onions.

*Did you know?*

The National Cancer Institute has endorsed a study which found that women who consume a lot of vegetables and fruits rich in beta-carotene (at least 5 per day) have a lower chance of getting cancer, including breast cancer.

# Corn Salsa

Serves 4 to 6

4 roma tomatoes, chopped

fresh kernels from 1 medium corn on the cob

⅓ cup cilantro, chopped

2 scallions, chopped

2 teaspoons marinated jalapeño peppers

½ teaspoon granulated date sugar

¼ teaspoon sea salt

½ cup cooked black-eyed peas (optional)

**Mix** all the ingredients in a medium-size bowl. Chill and serve with Baked Corn Tortilla Chips (page 128) or on top of burritos or enchiladas.

Per serving: Calories: 33, Protein: 1 gm., Fat: 0 gm., Carbohydrates: 7 gm.

# Carrots in Sweet Mustard Sauce

Serves 4

3 cups water

3 large carrots, cut into 1-inch pieces

1½ tablespoons brown rice syrup or honey

1 tablespoon water

2 teaspoons Dijon mustard

**In a medium saucepan**, add 3 cups water and the carrots, and bring to a boil. Lower the heat and cook on low for 20 minutes until tender.

**Drain** the carrots and reserve the cooking water for soup broth.

**In a small cup**, combine the brown rice syrup, 1 tablespoon water, and mustard.

**Pour** the sauce over the carrots, and stir to cover. Serve immediately.

Per serving: Calories: 46, Protein: 0 gm., Fat: 0 gm., Carbohydrates: 10 gm.

# Sweet Potato Casserole

Serves 6 to 8

**Scrub** the sweet potatoes and bake at 400° for 1 hour and 10 minutes.

**Remove** the sweet potatoes from the oven, and allow to cool slightly, at least until skin is not to hot to remove. Peel the sweet potatoes and mash them in a medium bowl.

**Add** the soymilk, oil, maple syrup, vanilla, nutmeg, and cinnamon, and mix well.

**Pour** the mixture into an oiled loaf pan and bake for 40 minutes. Serve this dish as a vegetable or a dessert.

Per serving: Calories: 194, Protein: 2 gm., Fat: 3 gm., Carbohydrates: 38 gm.

6 large sweet potatoes

¼ cup lite, vanilla soymilk or rice milk

2 tablespoons canola oil

2 tablespoons maple syrup

1 teaspoon vanilla extract

¼ teaspoon nutmeg

¼ teaspoon cinnamon

## Did you know?

One medium sweet potato or one large carrot provides the recommended daily allowance of 5 to 6 milligrams of beta carotene. It is estimated that the average American gets less than 1.5 milligrams a day.

# Garlic Greens

Serves 4

2 tablespoons water

4 cloves garlic, minced

½ red onion, chopped

1 pound collard greens, kale, or Swiss chard, cleaned, deveined, and chopped

1 teaspoon balsamic vinegar

1 teaspoon tamari

1 teaspoon water

2 teaspoons orange juice

**Place** 2 tablespoons water in a large skillet, add the garlic, and sauté 1 minute on medium-high heat.

**Add** the red onion and sauté for 2 more minutes.

**Mix** in the collards and cook for 5 more minutes.

**Turn** the heat to low, and cover.

**In a small bowl**, mix together the vinegar, tamari, water, and orange juice. Pour over the collards and mix.

**Cover** again and cook on low 15 more minutes until the greens are tender.

Per serving: Calories: 35, Protein: 2 gm., Fat: 0 gm., Carbohydrates: 7 gm.

## Did you know?

Eating greens is a wonderful way to help strengthen the liver.

## Did you know?

Greens are an important source of chlorophyll, a vital component for creating healthy red blood cells, the carriers of oxygen in the body. Chlorophyll also helps regulate the bowels, and promotes clear thinking. Greens are high in vitamins A and C and iron, and calcium.

# Cucumber Raita

Serves 3 to 4

**Peel**, seed, and dice the cucumber. (There is no need to peel the cucumber if it is organic.)

**Sprinkle** the cucumber with 1 teaspoon salt, and allow to set for 1 hour to extract the liquid. Rinse and pat dry.

**Place** the cumin seeds in a dry skillet, and roast over medium heat until the seeds turn darker. Transfer the seeds to a coffee bean grinder, and buzz briefly until the seeds are ground.

**Combine** the remaining ingredients and the roasted cumin in a blender or food processor, leaving some mint for garnish.

**In a serving bowl**, combine the blended ingredients with the cucumber, chill until ready to serve. Garnish with the remaining mint leaves. You can also combine the raita with chilled, cooked brown rice for an impromptu rice salad, spoon the sauce over a baked potato, or use as a dressing for the Mother Earth's Veggie Special (page 164).

Per serving: Calories: 122, Protein: 7 gm., Fat: 5 gm., Carbohydrates: 13 gm.

1 large cucumber

1½ teaspoons sea salt

1 teaspoon cumin seeds

⅛-¼ teaspoon red pepper flakes

1 cup plain soy yogurt

1 tablespoon lemon juice

2 tablespoons fresh mint leaves, or 1 teaspoon dry

# Mushroom and Green Pea Risotto

Serves 4

2 teaspoons olive oil

2 cloves garlic, minced

1 cup scallions, chopped

8 oz. mushrooms

1 teaspoon sea salt

1½ cups arborio rice

3½ cups water

2 tablespoons vegetable chicken broth

½ cup frozen peas

1 teaspoon basil

**In a medium-size saucepan**, heat the olive oil, add the garlic and scallions, and sauté on medium-high heat for about 2 minutes.

**Add** the mushrooms and sauté 2 more minutes.

**Sprinkle** the salt over the mushrooms.

**Stir** in the arborio rice, being sure to mix thoroughly, and sauté for 1 minute.

**In a small saucepan**, mix the water and vegetable broth and heat.

**Reduce** the heat to medium on the rice mixture, and slowly stir in the vegetable broth, ⅓ of a cup at a time, until all the liquid has been absorbed. Bure sure to stir constantly. The rice should be done in about 30 minutes and should be done al dente, like pasta.

**Add** the peas and basil toward the end of the cooking. Serve warm. Soy parmesan cheese can be sprinkled over the top of the rice and/or sprinkled over each serving.

Per serving: Calories: 229, Protein: 5 gm., Fat: 3 gm., Carbohydrates: 44 gm.

**Variation:** Omit the scallions, mushrooms, peas, and basil and add 1½ cups leeks (thoroughly cleaned, using the white and green parts), 1 cup butternut squash cut in ½ inch cubes, and ½ package (5 oz.) frozen, thawed, and drained spinach. Sauté the leeks with the garlic, add the squash, and sauté for 2 minutes before adding the liquid. Add the spinach during the last 15 minutes of the cooking time.

# Baked Potato Wedges

Serves 4

**Preheat** the oven to 400°.

**Cut** each potato lengthwise into 6 to 7 wedges.

**Dry** each wedge with a paper towel, and place in a medium-size bowl. Add the basil and olive oil, and mix well.

**Spray** a large baking sheet with canola spray, arrange the wedges in a single layer, and bake for 30 minutes. Remove from the oven and sprinkle the wedges with the cheese and seasonings.

**Place** the potatoes back in the oven, and bake 10 more minutes until browned and tender. Serve warm.

Per serving: Calories. 140, Protein. 3 gm., Fat: 1 gm., Carbohydrates: 28 gm.

3 large baking potatoes, peeled

½ teaspoon dried basil

extra virgin olive oil (drizzled over the potatoes)

2-3 tablespoons soy parmesan cheese

sea salt to taste

black pepper or kelp to taste

## Did you know?

To cut back on oil in your diet, fill a clean plastic spray bottle with your favorite cooking oil, and use to spray on pans, skillets, casseroles, etc.

# Stuffed Baked Potatoes

Serves 4

2 large russet baking potatoes

2 cups broccoli flowers

½ cup soymilk, plain

½ teaspoon each: onion powder, garlic powder, and thyme

⅛ teaspoon black pepper

paprika

2 tablespoons soy parmesan cheese

**Preheat** the oven to 400°.

**Scrub** the potatoes and bake for 40 to 50 minutes until tender.

**Remove** the potatoes from the oven, and let cool enough to handle. Slice them in half and scoop out the inside, leaving the skin as a shell to stuff. Mash the potatoes.

**Steam** the broccoli for about 10 to 12 minutes until tender.

**In a large mixing bowl**, mix the potatoes, broccoli, soymilk, onion powder, garlic powder, thyme, and black pepper.

**Lower** the oven to 350°.

**Fill** the potato shells with the potato mixture, and sprinkle the tops of the potatoes with paprika and ½ tablespoon soy parmesan cheese.

**Place** in a baking dish, and bake for about 20 minutes until heated through.

Per serving: Calories: 120, Protein: 4 gm., Fat: 1 gm., Carbohydrates: 23 gm.

## Did you know?

Potatoes are a powerhouse of complex carbohydrates. A 6 oz. potato provides almost twice as much potassium as a banana and about half the daily requirement of vitamin C. They should be stored in the dark to avoid developing green spots and excessive sprouting. They should not be stored with onions because of the gases they both give off.

# Oven Baked Hash Browns

Serves 4

**Steam** the potatoes for about 10 to 15 minutes until tender. Wash and drain. If desired, you can spray the potatoes with a spritz of olive oil.

**In a small bowl**, pour ¼ cup hot water over the textured vegetable protein, and let set 10 minutes.

**Preheat** the oven to 350°.

**In a medium-size saucepan**, sauté the onion, garlic, and red pepper for 5 minutes on medium heat in 1 tablespoon water. Add the tamari and black pepper, and sauté until tender.

**In a medium baking dish**, mix together the textured vegetable protein and sautéed vegetables, and bake for 30 minutes. Halfway through cooking, add 2 tablespoons water, and the potatoes, and mix.

2 pounds potatoes, peeled and diced

¼ cup hot water

¼ pound textured vegetable protein or seitan

1 medium onion, chopped

4 cloves garlic, chopped

1 cup red pepper, chopped

1 tablespoon water

1 tablespoon tamari

black pepper to taste (optional)

2 tablespoons water

Per serving: Calories: 319, Protein: 18 gm., Fat: 0 gm., Carbohydrates: 60 gm.

# Maine-Style Grilled Potatoes

Serves 8

3 large baking potatoes,
    scrubbed, peeled, and sliced

2 onions, chopped

2 teaspoons tamari

sea salt to taste

pepper to taste

**Place** the potatoes on a big enough piece of foil to fold up around the edges of the potatoes, and seal them for grilling.

**Spread** the onions on top of the potatoes. Pour 2 capfuls of the tamari over the potatoes, and sprinkle with sea salt and pepper. Close up the foil. Place on a hot grill, close the lid, and grill for about 20 to 25 minutes until tender. For those who really like a butter flavor, you can use canola spread as an alternative.

Per serving: Calories: 85, Protein: 2 gm., Fat: 0 gm., Carbohydrates: 19 gm.

# Spaghetti Squash

Serves 6 to 8

1 medium-size spaghetti squash

## Did you know?

Spaghetti squash has ⅓ the calories of pasta. The size of the squash determines the thickness of the strands. A smaller squash will yield a thinner more delicate thread. Look for a squash that is hard with a glossy yellow or cream color. If stored in a cool dry place, they can keep up to six weeks.

**Cut** the squash in half, and remove the seeds. Place the squash halves in 2 inches of water in a large skillet with the insides facing down.

**Bring** the water to a boil. Cover, lower the heat to medium, and steam for about 20 minutes until tender. (You can place 1 tablespoon of tamari in the water.)

**Season** with soy parmesan cheese, and serve warm or cold.

Per serving: Calories: 46, Protein: 1 gm., Fat: 0 gm., Carbohydrates: 10 gm.

**Variation:** Serve the spaghetti squash topped with your favorite spaghetti sauce with some whole basil leaves added to the sauce, and garnish with soy parmesan cheese.

# Roasted Red Potatoes

Serves 6

**Preheat** the oven to 350°.

**Clean** and chop the potatoes, leaving the skin on.

**Lightly coat** a baking sheet or pan with cooking spray, and spread the chopped potatoes on the baking sheet.

**Lightly spray** the potatoes with the olive oil.

**Sprinkle** the potatoes with the sea salt, black pepper, and rosemary, and bake for about 25 minutes until tender.

Per serving: Calories: 227, Protein: 3 gm., Fat: 1 gm., Carbohydrates: 51 gm.

6 red potatoes

olive oil spray

sea salt to taste

black pepper to taste

fresh or dry rosemary (optional)

## Did you know?

If you usually peel your potatoes, you may be losing most of the potassium. Sixty percent of the potassium that is found in a potato is under the skin. Potassium helps to neutralize acids in the body. Bernard Jensen's rich potassium broth is made by simmering the peelings from two potatoes in a pint of water for twenty minutes. Strain off the peelings, and drink the broth.

# Cabbage Stir-Fry

Serves 4

1 large onion, chopped

½ head green cabbage, coarsely
  chopped

3 tofu hot dogs, chopped

2 teaspoons tamari

1 teaspoon water

**Spray** a large skillet with canola mist, and sauté the onion on medium high heat for 3 to 4 minutes.

**Add** the cabbage and tofu hot dogs, and continue sautéing for about 5 minutes.

**Lower** the heat, add the tamari and water, cover with a lid, and continue to cook for approximately 10 more minutes until the cabbage is tender.

**Remove** the lid and cook 5 more minutes. Serve hot.

Per serving: Calories: 84, Protein: 7 gm., Fat: 10 gm., Carbohydrates: 11 gm.

**Variation:** Add ½ cup sauerkraut the last few minutes of cooking.

Per serving: Calories: 89, Protein: 7 gm., Fat: 2 gm., Carbohydrates: 11 gm.

## Did you know?

Cabbage is an excellent source of Vitamin C. Raw and cooked cabbage both contain a fair amount of Vitamin A. The outside leaves of cabbage may have as much as 40% more calcium than the inside leaves.

# Broiled Vegetable Medley

Serves 8

**Cut** the rutabaga and and turnips into 1-inch slices, then cut each slice into chunks. Cut the carrots into 4 long pieces, then cut each piece in half lengthwise. Place the red onion on one end, and slice from the top down into one inch slices.

**Place** the vegetables in a steamer, and steam for about 15 minutes until all the vegetables are tender. Spread the vegetables in a large baking dish (such as a lasagna pan).

**In a small mixing bowl**, mix the water, lemon juice, oil, lemon rind, vinegar, garlic and salt.

**Pour** the marinade over the vegetables, and chill for a few hours. If possible, let set overnight, being sure to occasionally stir the vegetables. Remove the vegetables from the marinade.

**Place** foil on a large baking sheet or pan, and spread the vegetables on the foil. Place the pan under a hot broiler, and broil for about 15 to 20 minutes until the vegetables are browned. Flip the vegetables every 2 to 3 minutes to be sure they don't burn. Serve warm with a green salad and muffin or hot bread.

1 large rutabaga, peeled

5 small to medium-size turnips, peeled

2 large carrots, peeled

1 medium red onion, peeled

½ cup water

¼ cup fresh lemon juice

¼ cup extra virgin olive oil

¾ tablespoon lemon rind, grated

2 tablespoons apple cider vinegar

2 cloves garlic, minced

2 teaspoons sea salt

Per serving: Calories: 98, Protein: 1 gm., Fat: 7 gm., Carbohydrates: 8 gm.

**Variation:** After steaming, serve the vegetables hot with your favorite herbal seasoning. Another option is to cook the vegetables on the grill instead of under the broiler.

# Marinated Cucumbers

Yield: 4 small servings

3 teaspoons flax oil

2 tablespoons brown rice vinegar

2 cucumbers, cut in rounds

**Mix** all the ingredients together, and let the cucumber marinate.

**Variation:** Use raspberry vinegar instead of brown rice vinegar.

Per serving: Calories: 53, Protein: 1 gm., Fat: 3 gm., Carbohydrates: 5 gm.

# Garlic Brussels Sprouts

Serves 6

1 (20 oz.) package. frozen Brussels sprouts

5 tablespoons water

1½ teaspoons soy sauce

1 teaspoon garlic powder

**In a large skillet**, sauté the Brussels sprouts in the water for about 10 minutes.

**Add** the soy sauce and garlic powder to the Brussels sprouts, and continue cooking about 5 to 10 more minutes until tender. Serve warm.

Per serving: Calories: 37, Protein: 1 gm., Fat: 0 gm., Carbohydrates: 7 gm.

# Vegetable Spring Rolls

Serves 6

**Combine** the carrots, scallions, tarragon, black pepper, water, tamari, mirin, and seitan. Mix well and let stand at least 30 minutes.

**Prior to cooking**, crush the noodles with a rolling pin. Boil for 2 minutes or soak for 10 minutes in hot water. Rinse and drain.

**Fill** a large bowl with warm water. Dip each rice-paper round into the water for about 10 seconds until softened and translucent. Transfer to a piece of waxed paper.

**Place** about 2 tablespoons noodles and 2 tablespoons vegetables along the lower edge of the rice paper, about 1 inch from the edge. Fold the bottom of the paper over the filling, fold in both sides, and roll into a tight cylinder. Cover with plastic wrap, and chill for 30 minutes.

**Serve** the spring rolls with a dipping sauce made of equal parts of tamari and water and some wasabi (Japanese horseradish). For a hot mustard sauce, combine 2 tablespoons dry mustard and two tablespoons water. For a sweet and sour sauce, whisk together ¼ cup sugar-free apricot preserves, 1 teaspoon reduced-sodium soy sauce, 1 teaspoon spicy mustard, 1 teaspoon apple cider vinegar, and 1 teaspoon water.

Per serving: Calories: 318, Protein: 8 gm., Fat: 0 gm., Carbohydrates: 72 gm.

**Variation:** Substitute ½ cup textured vegetable protein, soaked for 10 minutes in ½ cup hot water, for the seitan.

2 large carrots, grated

2 scallions, diced

1 teaspoon dried tarragon

¼ teaspoon ground black pepper

1-2 teaspoons each: water, tamari, and mirin

1 cup ground seitan (spicy is best)

2 cups cooked mung bean thread noodles

16 (6-inch) rice paper rounds

*About this recipe*——

Rice paper rounds can be found in oriental markets and are great for those allergic to wheat products.

# Japanese Soba Noodles with Steamed Vegetables

Serves 4 to 6

2 cups water

1 strip kombu

1 tablespoon fresh gingerroot, grated

1½ tablespoons tamari soy sauce

2 tablespoons mirin

2 green onions, chopped

2 carrots, cut into circles

1 small bunch of broccoli flowers, chopped

1 small bunch bok choy, chopped

1 package Japanese soba noodles

black sesame seeds (optional)

1 sheet nori seaweed, cut into thin strips (optional)

**To prepare** the soba noodle broth for the noodles, place the water and kombu in a small pot, bring to a boil, and boil for about 5 minutes.

**Put** the gingerroot in a cheesecloth, and squeeze out the juice.

**Turn** the heat to low, remove the strip of kombu, and add the tamari, mirin, green onions, and gingerroot juice, and cover until ready to use.

**In a large steamer**, steam the carrots and broccoli for about 10 minutes.

**Add** the bok choy to the steaming vegetables, and steam 5 more minutes until all the vegetables are crisp tender.

**Cook** the noodles according to the package directions. (Boil about 8 minutes, run under cold water, and drain.)

**Place** a mound of noodles on dinner plates with sides. Top with an assortment of the steamed vegetables, and pour about ¼ cup of the broth over the vegetables and noodles. Garnish with black sesame seeds, or nori, if desired.

Per serving: Calories: 196, Protein: 6 gm., Fat: 1 gm., Carbohydrates: 40 gm.

Hot Cha Cha Entrees

# Zucchini Lasagne

### Serves 9

1 pound firm or extra firm tofu

1½ tablespoons light miso

1 clove garlic, minced

8 oz. frozen spinach, thawed
    and well drained

3 tablespoons water

2 cloves garlic, minced

1 medium onion, chopped

½ cup red pepper, chopped

1 cup mushrooms, sliced

1 cup zucchini, chopped

2 cups broccoli stems and
    flowers, chopped

1 teaspoon oregano

½ teaspoon each: basil and
    thyme

1 teaspoon sea salt

4 cups tomato sauce

½ cup raw bulgur

9 lasagna noodles, cooked
    al dente

**Preheat** the oven to 350°.

**Place** the tofu in a steamer, and steam for 10 minutes.

**Place** the tofu, miso, and 1 clove garlic in a food processor, and pulse to a ricotta-like consistency. Add the spinach and pulse for 1 minute until blended.

**Place** 3 tablespoons of water in a large skillet, and sauté 2 cloves garlic and the onion for 2 minutes. Add the red pepper, mushrooms, zucchini, and broccoli, cover, and simmer about 6 to 8 minutes. Add more water if necessary.

**Remove** the lid and add the herbs. If liquid is left in the pan, turn the heat to high for 1 or 2 minutes to evaporate.

**In a medium-size bowl,** mix together the tomato sauce and bulgur.

**Lightly oil** the bottom of a 9 x 13-inch lasagna pan, and spread 1 cup of the tomato sauce on the bottom of the dish.

**Place** 3 noodles on top of the sauce, and spread ½ of the tofu mixture then ½ of the vegetables on top.

**Repeat** with a second layer, starting with 1 cup sauce, the remaining ½ of the tofu mixture and vegetables.

**Cover** with 1 more cup of sauce, 3 noodles, and then the remaining cup of sauce.

**Cover** with foil and bake for 25 minutes. Uncover for the last 5 minutes of cooking. Cool slightly before cutting.

Per serving: Calories: 232, Protein: 11 gm., Fat: 4 gm.,
    Carbohydrates: 39 gm.

**Variation:** Omit the broccoli and substitute eggplant.

# Stuffed Peppers

Yield: 4 peppers

**Prepare** the bulgur by placing 1 cup bulgur in a medium size bowl and adding 1 cup boiling water. Let set for approximately 1 hour.

**Wash** the green peppers, cut off the tops, remove the stems, and chop up the tops. Clean the seeds and extra pulp out of the peppers. Place in a steamer basket, and steam for about 12 minutes until tender.

**Preheat** the oven to 350°.

**In a large skillet**, sauté the chopped green peppers, mushrooms, celery, and onions in the water.

**Add** the corn, beans, and seasonings.

**Mix** the bulgur with the vegetables and seasonings.

**Fill** up the pepper shells, place in a baking dish, and cover with the tomato juice.

**Bake** for 20 to 30 minutes.

Per pepper: Calories: 234, Protein: 9 gm., Fat: 0 gm., Carbohydrates: 47 gm.

**Variation:** Sprinkle the top with grated soy cheddar cheese.

1 cup bulgur, or 1½ cups cooked rice

4 green, red, or yellow peppers

¼ cup green peppers, chopped (from the tops)

½ cup mushrooms, sliced

¼ cup (1 stick) celery, chopped

½ cup onions, chopped

3-4 tablespoons water or vegetable broth

½ cup frozen corn

1 cup cooked pinto beans, (4 oz. mashed)

2 teaspoons tamari

½ teaspoon sea salt

1 teaspoon garlic powder

½ teaspoon black pepper

2 cups spicy tomato juice

## Did you know?

Indoles (phytochemicals) are found in legumes. They increase the activity of enzymes that may help make the hormone estrogen less effective, which could reduce the risk of breast cancer.

# Broccoli Casserole

Serves 6 to 8

1 large bunch broccoli stems
   and flowers, chopped

12 oz. Cream of Mushroom
   Soup (page 172), or 1 can
   cream of mushroom soup

1½ teaspoons egg replacer
   + 2 tablespoons water

½ cup tofu or eggless
   mayonnaise

1 cup soy cheddar cheese,
   grated

1 small onion, grated

2 slices whole wheat bread

¼ teaspoon onion powder

pinch each: sea salt, black
   pepper, and paprika

**Steam** the broccoli for about 10 to 12 minutes, and drain.

**In a large mixing bowl**, mix the broccoli, soup, egg replacer mix, tofu, cheese, and onion. Place the broccoli mixture in a casserole dish.

**Preheat** the oven to 350°.

**Using** the crumb setting on a blender, prepare a bread crumb topping by blending together the bread, onion powder, salt, black pepper, and paprika.

**Sprinkle** the bread crumbs over the top of the casserole, and drizzle 2 tablespoons of water over the top of the bread crumbs.

**Bake** for 30 minutes.

Per serving: Calories: 203, Protein: 5 gm., Fat: 13 gm., Carbohydrates: 14 gm.

**Variation:** You can spritz the bread crumbs with oil using a small plastic sprayer bottle filled with oil.

# Whole Grain Croutons

Serves 6 to 8

**Preheat** the oven to 250°.

**Remove** the crusts from the bread, and dab the oil on with a pastry brush. Cut the bread into ½-inch cubes. Combine the herbs and garlic powder in a plastic container with a lid, add the bread cubes, cover, and shake to coat. Bake the bread cubes on a cookie sheet for 20 minutes until crisp.

Per serving: Calories: 37, Protein: 1 gm., Fat: 2 gm., Carbohydrates: 3 gm.

**Variation:** Use rye instead of whole grain bread, and top with crushed caraway seeds and dry mustard.

2 slices whole wheat bread, cubed

1 tablespoon olive oil

¼ teaspoon each: basil and oregano

dash garlic powder

## About this recipe—

You can make whole grain croutons and grind them up for topping.

## Did you know?

Insoluble fiber, found in wheat bran, is beneficial to the digestive system. It helps prevent problems such as diverticulosis, constipation, and may help reduce the risk of colon cancer.

# Broccoli-Mushroom Quiche

Serves 6 to 8

1 cup yellow squash, grated

½ cup carrots, grated

2 tablespoons water

½ cup parsnips, grated

⅔ cup whole wheat pastry flour

pinch of sea salt

1 cup zucchini, grated

1 tablespoon vegetable broth
   or water

4 cloves garlic, minced

12 oz. mushrooms, thinly sliced

1 teaspoon dried basil

1 teaspoon dried oregano

1 cup small broccoli flowers

1 pound firm or soft low-fat
   tofu

1 tablespoon umeboshi vinegar

2 tablespoons water

½ teaspoon sea salt

freshly ground black pepper

paprika

**Preheat** the oven to 375°.

**To make the crust**, sprinkle the yellow squash with sea salt, let set for 15 minutes, and squeeze out the liquid.

**Mix** the squash, carrots, water, parsnips, flour, salt, and zucchini together.

**Press** into the bottom and sides of an oiled 9-inch (or deep dish) pie pan.

**Pre-bake** for 45 minutes.

**Reduce** the oven to 350°.

**Heat** a large skillet over medium heat, and add the broth.

**Sauté** the garlic for 15 seconds, add the mushrooms, and sauté over low heat, stirring, for 3 to 4 minutes.

**Sprinkle** on the basil and oregano, add the broccoli, cover, and steam 2 more minutes. Remove from the heat.

**Steam** the tofu for 10 minutes, and drain.

**Place** the tofu, vinegar, water, and salt in a blender or food processor, and blend until smooth and creamy. Add black pepper to taste.

**Gently fold** the mushrooms and broccoli into the creamy tofu. Pour into the pre-baked pie shell, and sprinkle on the paprika.

**Bake** for 30 minutes or until the tofu ridges take on a slightly beige hue. Cool and serve.

Per serving: Calories: 143, Protein: 10 gm., Fat: 3 gm., Carbohydrates: 18 gm.

**Variation:** Try combining other varieties of fresh mushrooms, such as shiitake, porcini, or chanterelles for half of the mushrooms.

# Mexican Tamale Pie

Serves 6 to 8

**In a large skillet**, sauté the green pepper in the water.

**In a small bowl**, mix the textured vegetable protein and hot water, and let set for about 10 minutes.

**Add** the soaked textured vegetable protein to the skillet, along with the soup mix, tomatoes, tomato sauce, corn, olives, maple syrup, garlic, and paprika.

**Simmer** all the ingredients together for 15 to 20 minutes, and place in medium-size casserole dish.

**Preheat** the oven to 375°.

**In a medium-size saucepan**, cook the cornmeal, water, and salt for about 10 minutes until thick, stirring constantly.

**Spread** the cornmeal topping on top of the casserole mixture, and bake for 40 minutes.

Per serving: Calories: 207, Protein: 14 gm., Fat: 2 gm., Carbohydrates: 32 gm.

**Variation:** Add 1 cup grated soy cheddar cheese and 1 teaspoon chili powder to the casserole mixture.

1 medium green pepper, chopped

2 tablespoons water

2 cups textured vegetable protein

2 cups hot water

1 package natural onion soup mix

2 cups canned tomatoes

8 oz. tomato sauce

1½ cups corn kernels

½ cup black olives, cut in half

1 tablespoon maple syrup

¾ teaspoon garlic

1 teaspoon paprika

¾ cup cornmeal

1 cup cold water

½ teaspoon sea salt

# Leftovers Quiche

Yield: one 9-inch quiche (serves 6 to 8)

1 teaspoon canola oil, canola
    spray, or vegetable broth

½ cup onion, diced

1 cup (6 oz.) mushrooms, diced

1½ cups leftover vegetables,
    (broccoli, asparagus, etc.)

½ teaspoon salt

¼ cup water

1 (10.5 oz) package lite firm
    tofu

½ teaspoon sea salt

1 tablespoon tamari

1 teaspoon curry powder (see
    note)

1 teaspoon cumin (see note)

½ cup water

2 cups cooked rice

¼ teaspoon paprika

## About this recipe——

This quiche is very versatile and is limited only by what remains in the fridge from last night's dinner. By varying the grain in the crust, the veggies and spices, you can create new and exciting tastes every time. Try the tofu cream sauce on pasta or baked potatoes!

**Preheat** the oven to 350°.

**Heat** a medium-sized skillet on medium heat, add the oil, and sauté the onion for 2 minutes.

**Add** the mushrooms and leftover vegetables, sprinkle with ½ teaspoon salt, and add ¼ cup water.

**Cover** and cook until tender but colorful, about 5 to 10 minutes, depending upon which vegetables you use.

**In a food processor** or blender, combine the tofu, ½ teaspoon salt, the tamari, curry powder, and cumin. Gradually add up to ½ cup water to make blending easy.

**Combine** the vegetables with the tofu cream sauce, and blend well.

**Press** the rice into a lightly oiled pie plate.

**Transfer** the tofu-vegetable mix to the rice crust pan, smooth the surface, and sprinkle with paprika.

**Bake** about 30 minutes until nicely golden. Allow to cool for 10 minutes before cutting. This recipe tastes completely different and equally delicious cold.

**Variation:** Try varying the spices as follows: Italian—basil and oregano; rosemary and marjoram or sage; French—thyme and rosemary or tarragon. If fresh spices are available, double or triple the amount required.

**Variation:** Use 3 cups of leftover cooked grain. If you're using different grains, be sure that you mix a small portion of a glutinous grain, such as as millet or amaranth with your rice. This will help the crust stick together. It is helpful to periodically dip your fingers in water while forming the rice crust to prevent the rice from sticking to your fingers.

Per serving: Calories: 123, Protein: 6 gm., Fat: 6 gm.,
    Carbohydrates: 21 gm.

# Polenta with Pinto Beans

Serves 6 to 8

**Sauté** the onion and garlic in the oil for about 5 minutes until tender.

**Add** the carrot and sauté 5 more minutes.

**Add** the beans and simmer about 10 more minutes until the carrots are tender. Keep warm while preparing the polenta.

**In a large saucepan,** bring the water and salt to a boil. Slowly pour in the cornmeal, stirring continuously with a wire whisk.

**Continue** to cook over medium heat until the cornmeal thickens, about 5 minutes. Reduce the heat to low, cover, and continue to cook for 20 minutes, stirring occasionally to prevent the mixture from sticking to the bottom of the pan.

**Place** a cup of the hot polenta in the bottom of a soup bowl, and top with the pinto bean mixture. Leftover polenta can be poured into a baking pan and refrigerated. You can cut it into squares the next day. It can be eaten plain, but is also delicious with a topping of real maple or brown rice syrup.

1 medium onion, chopped

2 cloves garlic, minced, or ¼ teaspoon garlic powder

½ teaspoon sesame oil

1 medium carrot, chopped

1 (15 oz.) can pinto beans with liquid

7 cups water

¾ teaspoon sea salt

2 cups yellow cornmeal or polenta

Per serving: Calories: 242, Protein: 8 gm., Fat: 1 gm., Carbohydrates: 49 gm.

# Vegetarian Chili

Serves 6

1 pound tofu, frozen

¼ cup water

2 tablespoons fruit-juice-
   sweetened ketchup

2 tablespoons tamari

1 tablespoon peanut butter

⅛ teaspoon garlic powder

1 large onion, chopped

2 cloves garlic, minced

1 teaspoon canola oil

2 (15 oz.) cans pinto beans,
   rinsed and drained

1½ tablespoons chili powder

1 tablespoon cumin

**Thaw** the tofu, squeeze dry, and crumble into a small bowl.

**To make** a marinade, combine the water, ketchup, tamari, peanut butter, and garlic powder.

**Pour** the marinade over the tofu, mix well, and refrigerate at least 1 hour.

**In a large, heavy-bottomed pot**, sauté the onion and garlic in the oil until the onion is transparent.

**Add** the marinated tofu and sauté 2 more minutes.

**Add** the pinto beans, chili powder, and cumin, and simmer for 5 minutes. Serve over long grain brown rice or with tortilla chips.

Per serving: Calories: 294, Protein: 17 gm., Fat: 6 gm., Carbohydrates: 43 gm.

# Linda's Squash Casserole

Serves 6

1 large onion, chopped

6 yellow crook neck squash, cut
   in rounds

¼ cup water

1½ teaspoons egg replacer + 2
   tablespoons water

1 cup soy cheddar cheese,
   grated

½ cup Italian bread crumbs

**Preheat** the oven to 350°.

**In a large skillet**, sauté the onion and squash in the water until cooked through.

**Stir** in the egg replacer mix, soy cheese, and ¼ cup of the bread crumbs.

**Spoon** into a medium-size casserole dish, and sprinkle with the remaining ¼ cup bread crumbs.

**Bake** for about 30 minutes.

Per serving: Calories: 156, Protein: 5 gm., Fat: 7 gm., Carbohydrates: 18 gm.

# Baked Tofu Nuggets

Yield: 36 nuggets

**Drain** the tofu and slice in half horizontally. Place the two slices on a large plate or cutting board covered with 2 to 3 paper towels. Then place 2 more paper towels on top. Set a heavy cast iron skillet weighted down with a heavy object on top to press the tofu. Let the tofu set for at least 30 minutes.

**To freeze** the tofu, place the two slices of tofu on a rack and place in the freezer. Leave in the freezer about 48 hours. The tofu will take on a yellow to amber color. If you leave the tofu in the freezer longer, place in a freezer bag.

**To defrost** the tofu, place the slices in a large bowl, and cover with hot boiling water, and let set for about 10 minutes.

**Drain** the tofu, and repeat step number 1 again to press the remaining water out of the tofu. This time press for only 20 minutes.

**Cut** the tofu slices in half, and cut each half in thirds. Turn lengthwise and cut into thirds again.

**Preheat** the oven to 350°.

**Mix** the ketchup and tamari. Dip the nuggets completely into the mixture, and place on an oiled cookie sheet.

**Bake** for 20 minutes, turning over once half way through baking.

If you don't have the time to freeze the tofu, you can skip the freezing step. Just press the water out of the tofu, cut into cubes, flavor, and bake at 350° for 30 minutes.

1 pound extra firm tofu

⅓ cup ketchup

2 tablespoons tamari

Per nugget: Calories: 12, Protein: 1 gm., Fat: 0 gm., Carbohydrates: 1 gm.

**Variation:** You can also dip the nuggets into a mixture of equal parts water and tamari and then dip into crushed almonds.

# Marinated Baked Tofu Nuggets

Serves 8

**Marinating Sauce:**

¼ cup tamari

1-2 tablespoons tahini

¼ cup water

¼ cup maple syrup

2 tablespoons brown rice
  vinegar

**To make the marinade**, mix the tamari, tahini, water, maple syrup, and vinegar.

**Make** tofu cubes by following the directions for Baked Tofu Nuggets. Instead of using a dip, let the tofu set for at least 1 hour in the marinade to absorb the flavors. Drain, reserving the marinade for future use.

**Instead of nuggets**, the tofu can also be sliced into 4 steaks, pressed, and marinated.

**For cooking** cubes or steaks, place on a lightly oiled baking sheet, and ladle a small amount of marinade over the tofu. Bake at 400° for 8 to 10 minutes until browned.

Per serving (8 servings): Calories: 49, Protein: 1 gm., Fat: 2 gm., Carbohydrates: 8 gm.

**Variation:** You can add some red pepper flakes, hot sauce or hot pepper oil to the marinade mixture to spice it up.

**Variation:** To make an apricot marinade for tofu nuggets, mix ¾ cup apricot preserves (or orange marmalade), ¼ cup vegetable broth, 2 tablespoons lemon juice, and 1 teaspoon dry mustard.

**Variation:** Marinate the tofu cubes for a few minutes in 2 tablespoons tamari, 1 tablespoon water, ½ tablespoon dill, and 2 cloves garlic, crushed. Bake at 350° for 20 minutes, baste, turn, and bake another 20 minutes. These can be used as croutons.

# Oriental Mushrooms with Tofu

Serves 4

**Drain** the tofu, press out the water, and cut into cubes.

**To make a marinade**, combine the water, tamari, lemon juice, and garlic powder.

**Add** the tofu cubes, cover the container with a lid, and rotate until all the tofu is coated with marinade. Place in the refrigerator and turn over every 10 minutes. Let marinate at least 20 minutes for absorbing the flavors of the marinade (the longer, the better).

**In a large skillet**, sauté the red onion, garlic, and gingerroot in the oil for a few minutes.

**Add** the mushrooms and water, and sauté for about 5 more minutes until softened, stirring occasionally.

**Sprinkle** the flour over the mixture until the mushrooms are coated.

**In a small bowl**, mix together the vegetable stock, tamari, and mirin, and pour over the mushrooms. Cook over medium heat about 4 minutes.

**Drain** the marinated tofu cubes. In a small skillet sprayed with canola mist, lightly sauté the tofu for about 5 minutes.

**Gently add** the tofu to the mushroom mixture, and cook 2 to 3 more minutes until warmed through. Serve over rice or other grains.

½ pound extra-firm tofu

1 tablespoon water

1 tablespoon tamari

1 tablespoon lemon juice

¼ teaspoon garlic powder

⅛ cup red onion, diced

2 cloves garlic minced

½-inch fresh gingerroot, grated

2 teaspoons toasted sesame oil

8 oz. package fresh
   mushrooms, cleaned, stems
   cut off

1 tablespoon water

1 tablespoon brown rice flour
   or whole wheat flour

½ cup vegetable stock

½ tablespoon tamari

½ tablespoon mirin

Per serving: Calories: 99, Protein: 6 gm., Fat: 1 gm.,
   Carbohydrates: 7 gm.

**Variation:** Sprinkle with ¼ cup toasted, slivered almonds.

# Marinated Broiled Tofu

Serves 4

1 pound extra firm tofu

¼ cup tamari

¼ cup water

⅛ cup fresh lemon juice

¼ cup red onion, minced

¼ cup brown rice syrup or
   honey

2½ cloves garlic, minced

1 teaspoon fresh gingerroot,
   minced

**Drain** the tofu, press out the water, and cut into 8 slices.

**To make the marinade** combine the tamari, water, lemon juice, red onion, rice syrup, garlic, and ginger-root in a covered jar or container, and shake well.

**Arrange** the tofu slices in a baking dish, such as a lasagna dish, and cover with the marinade. Let the tofu marinate for about 4 hours for the best flavor. You can marinate the tofu for a much shorter period of time, if desired.

**Coat** a baking sheet with oil, and arrange the tofu slices. Cover with some of the marinade. Make sure to get some of the chopped red onion, garlic, and ginger on each slice.

**Broil** for about 3 minutes on each side, being careful not to burn the tofu. Serve with a cooked grain and the Carrot and Sea Plant Salad (page 166), or make a sandwich with sprouts lettuce and cumbers.

Per serving: Calories: 170, Protein: 10 gm., Fat: 5 gm., Carbohydrates: 21 gm.

## Did you know?

Soybeans, the primary ingredient in tofu, may be a strong fighter against breast cancer. Soybeans mimic the action of tamoxifen, a drug commonly used to treat breast tumors.

# Mom's Mashed Potato Casserole

Serves 8

**Spray** the inside of a large, round baking dish with canola spray. Place the corn on the bottom of the dish.

**Spray** a large skillet with canola spray, and sauté the onion and textured vegetable protein on medium heat for 10 minutes.

**Add** the cumin, garlic powder, paprika, onion powder, and tamari to the mixture, and continue cooking for 10 more minutes on medium heat.

**Spread** the textured vegetable protein mixture over the corn.

**Preheat** the oven to 350°.

**Prepare** the mashed potatoes according to the package directions.

**Spread** the mashed potatoes over the top of the textured vegetable protein mixture to cover. Bake, covered, for 20 minutes. Remove the cover and bake 10 more minutes. Serve warm. Season with sea salt or herbal seasoning to taste.

1 (16 oz.) package frozen corn, cooked according to package directions

1 large onion, chopped

1½ cups textured vegetable protein soaked in 1½ cups hot water for 5 minutes

2 teaspoons cumin

1 teaspoon garlic powder

1 teaspoon paprika

½ teaspoon onion powder

2 tablespoons tamari

2 cups instant mashed potatoes (made with soymilk)

Per serving: Calories: 268, Protein: 10 gm., Fat: 0 gm., Carbohydrates: 54 gm.

# Vegetable Pizza with Whole Wheat Crust

Serves 6

1 tablespoon dry baking yeast

¼ cup warm water

¾ cup water

2 tablespoons olive oil

¼ cup cornmeal

¼ cup sesame seeds

1½ cups whole wheat flour

1½ cups wheat pastry flour

¼ cup tofu, mashed

2 cups tomato sauce

1 teaspoon basil

1 teaspoon oregano

2 onions, sliced

1 red pepper, chopped

1 yellow pepper, chopped

1 cup mushrooms, chopped

soy mozzarella cheese, grated
   (optional)

**In a large mixing bowl**, mix the yeast and ¼ cup warm water, and let stand for 5 minutes.

**Add** ¾ cup water, the olive oil, cornmeal, sesame seeds, whole wheat flour, pastry flour, and tofu to the the yeast mixture. Knead the dough for 5 minutes until smooth and elastic. Cover and let rise 1 hour.

**Preheat** the oven to 400°.

**Oil** a cookie sheet with olive oil, and roll out the pizza dough on the sheet. Push up the sides of the dough.

**Spray** the dough with olive oil cooking spray, and spread on a thin layer of your favorite tomato sauce.

**Sprinkle** the basil and oregano over the pizza.

**In a large nonstick skillet**, sauté the onions, peppers, and mushrooms for about 5 minutes. Spread the vegetables on top of the pizza.

**Top** with the soy cheese, and bake for 20 to 25 minutes.

Per serving: Calories: 352, Protein: 11 gm., Fat: 9 gm., Carbohydrates: 56 gm.

## Did you know?

The outer hulls of grape seeds contain tartaric acid, also known as cream of tartar. Just a little bit of cream of tartar added to your diet helps break down mucus in the body.

# Mock a La King

Serves 6

**Dry roast** the whole wheat pastry flour in a medium-size skillet on medium-high temperature.

**Slowly add** the rice milk, stirring constantly for about 3 to 4 minutes on high heat. Once the mixture begins to boil, lower the heat, and continue to stir until thickened, about 5 to 10 minutes.

**Add** the mixed vegetables, seitan, spices, and pimentos.

**Cook** 15 more minutes until the vegetables are cooked. This can be served over brown rice or whole grain toast. For those who like more sauce, you can reduce the seitan or mixed vegetables to 1 cup.

Per serving: Calories: 111, Protein: 14 gm., Fat: 1 gm., Carbohydrates: 12 gm.

**Variation:** This same mixture could be used in leftovers to make a quick pot pie. Instead of a whole wheat crust, try using pieces of phyllo dough to cover the mixture for something quick and easy.

2 tablespoons whole wheat pastry flour

2 cups low-fat rice or soymilk

1-1½ cups frozen mixed vegetables

1½ cups chicken style seitan, cut into cubes

¼-½ teaspoon black pepper

½ teaspoon sea salt or to taste

¼ teaspoon garlic powder

¼ teaspoon thyme

2 tablespoons of pimentos (optional)

*Did you know?*

Certain compounds in soy have been shown to inhibit the growth of breast cancer cells.

# Vegetarian Goulash

Serves 8

8 oz. pasta shells

1 cup textured vegetable
protein

1 cup hot water

1 green pepper, chopped

1 medium onion, chopped

2 tablespoons water

1 (16 oz.) can chopped
tomatoes

3 tablespoons tomato paste
mixed with 4 tablespoons
water

2 tablespoons tamari

2 tablespoons fruit-juice-
sweetened ketchup

½ teaspoon dried basil

½ teaspoon paprika

**Cook** the pasta according to package directions, drain, and rinse.

**In a small bowl**, mix the textured vegetable protein and hot water, and let set for 5 minutes.

**Spray** a large skillet with canola mist, and sauté the textured vegetable protein for about 5 minutes on medium-high heat. Remove from the pan and set aside.

**Clean** out the skillet and spray again with canola mist. Turn the heat to medium-high, and sauté the green pepper and onion for 5 minutes.

**Add** 2 tablespoons water and sauté 5 more minutes until the green peppers are tender.

**Lower** the heat, add the textured vegetable protein, and gently mix in the pasta, tomatoes, tomato paste mixture, tamari, ketchup, basil, and paprika.

**Cook** for about 10 to 15 minutes until warmed through, and serve.

Per serving: Calories: 93, Protein: 7 gm., Fat: 0 gm.,
Carbohydrates: 15 gm.

# Seitan Pot Roast with Vegetables

Yield: 1 pot roast (serves 6 to 8)

**Mix** the seitan mix with the nutritional yeast, black pepper, ½ teaspoon garlic powder, and parsley. Add 2 cups water and the tamari, and mix well. Knead for 5 minutes, and form into an oval loaf.

**Preheat** the oven to 350°.

**Make** a broth by mixing 5 cups water, 2 tablespoons tamari, the onion powder, ½ teaspoon garlic powder, and kombu.

**Place** the gluten roast in a deep baking pan, and cover with the broth. Cook uncovered for 30 minutes.

**Take out**, turn the seitan loaf over gently, and add the carrots, onions, and potatoes.

**Cover** and bake another 2 to 2½ hours until very firm throughout.

Per serving: Calories: 285, Protein: 36 gm., Fat: 1 gm., Carbohydrates: 33 gm.

**Variation:** For a German pot roast, reduce the water by ⅓ cup in the broth, and add ⅓ cup apple cider vinegar, ⅓ cup catsup, ⅓ cup vegetarian Worcestershire sauce, ¼ teaspoon ginger, ¼ teaspoon cinnamon, ⅛ teaspoon cloves, and ⅛ teaspoon nutmeg.

2 cups quick seitan mix

1½ tablespoons nutritional yeast

½ teaspoon black pepper

½ teaspoon garlic powder

½ teaspoon parsley

2 cups water

2 tablespoons tamari

5 cups water

2 tablespoons tamari

½ teaspoon onion powder

½ teaspoon garlic powder

2 sticks kombu (optional)

6 carrots, cut in long slices

2 onions, cut in chunks

4 potatoes, cut in large pieces

*About this recipe—*

This pot roast can be sliced for sandwiches. It can also be cut in chunks and mixed with barbecue sauce, a great accompaniment to potato salad.

# Browned Tofu or Tempeh

## Serves 8

1 pound extra-firm tofu or
    tempeh
¼ cup + 2 tablespoons tamari

**Steam** the tofu or tempeh for about 15 minutes, then cool. If using the tofu, drain and squeeze out the excess water.

**Cut** the tofu into bite size cubes. Place the tamari in a large skillet, and add the tofu.

**Brown** on medium-high heat with the lid on for about 10 minutes until all the liquid is absorbed.

Per serving: Calories: 51, Protein: 5 gm., Fat: 2 gm., Carbohydrates: 2 gm.

# Vegetable Tofu Stir Fry

## Serves 8

2 yellow onions, chopped
2 cloves garlic, chopped
3 to 4 tablespoons water
1½ cups red pepper, chopped
1 green or yellow pepper,
    chopped
1 medium head broccoli (stems
    and flowers), chopped
2 cups cauliflower, chopped
¼ cup water
1 full teaspoon ginger

**In a large skillet**, sauté the onions and garlic in 3 to 4 tablespoons water.

**Add** the red and green peppers, broccoli, cauliflower, ¼ cup water, and ginger, cover with a lid, and steam until tender.

**To serve**, place ½ cup of the vegetable mixture on top of ½ cup of Indian Rice (page 69) and garnish with reduced-sodium soy sauce, nutritional yeast, and if desired about 1 tablespoon of flax oil. Top with ⅛ cup of the Browned Tofu (page 120).

Per serving: Calories: 36, Protein: 1 gm., Fat: 0 gm., Carbohydrates: 7 gm.

# Healthful Snacks and Festive Fruits

# Smart Snacking

Snacking is an important part of a child's diet. Put some planning into your child's snacks so that good nutrition is not being compromised with junk food. Be sure you always have nutritious snacks in the house. This will help avoid the temptation to go for high-fat, empty-calorie foods. Here are some suggestions:

oil-free, air-popped popcorn

whole grain crackers

rice cakes spread with your favorite nut butter

whole wheat tortillas spread with peanut butter or almond butter (You can also drizzle with them with rice syrup or maple syrup and cinnamon, and/or sliced bananas)

lard-free bean dips—See Dip Suggestions (page 154)

low-salt whole wheat pretzels

non-fat soy yogurt

fresh fruit—apple and orange slices, bananas, strawberries, kiwi, grapes, cantaloupe, etc. (see Fruit Kabobs page 151)

raw vegetable sticks—carrots, zucchini, celery, etc.—See Vegetable Kabobs (page 152)

pita pockets stuffed with tofu cubes and vegetables

cold baked sweet potatoes

natural instant soups

roasted sunflower and pumpkin seeds

bagels

sugar-free puddings

instant brown rice pudding—heat up leftover brown rice with soy or rice milk, raisins, and cinnamon

cold fruit soup—plain soy yogurt blended with your favorite fruit

whole grain, sugar-free cereals with low-fat soy or rice milk.

dried fruits (Dr. Bernard Jensen, in *Foods that Heal*, recommends that dried fruit be soaked before eating.) Put the dried fruit in a pot of water, bring the water to a boil, turn off the heat, and let the fruit soak overnight.

# Carrot Raisin Muffins

Makes 12 to 14 large muffins

**Preheat** the oven to 350°.

**Soak** the raisins in hot water for 10 minutes, and drain.

**Combine** the flour, baking soda, cinnamon, nutmeg, and salt, and stir well.

**In a large bowl,** combine the dehydrated cane juice sweetener, oil, applesauce, egg replacer, orange juice, orange zest, and vanilla.

**Stir** in the flour mixture, and add the carrots, raisins, and pineapple with juice.

**Prepare** a 12-cup muffin tin with unbleached paper liners, and fill each cup ¾ full.

**Bake** for 20 to 25 minutes until a toothpick inserted into the center, comes out clean.

**Allow** the muffins to cool. Ice with Tofu Cream Cheese Frosting (page 34), if desired.

Per muffin: Calories: 155, Protein: 3 gm., Fat: 2 gm., Carbohydrates: 31 gm.

½ cup raisins

2 cups whole wheat pastry flour

2 teaspoons baking soda

½-1 teaspoon cinnamon

½ teaspoon nutmeg

⅛ teaspoon sea salt

¾ cup dehydrated cane juice sweetener or brown sugar

2 tablespoons canola oil

1 tablespoon applesauce

egg replacer for 2 eggs

½ cup orange juice

grated zest of 1 orange

2 teaspoons vanilla

2 cups shredded carrots

1 (8oz.) can unsweetened, crushed pineapple

# Apple Oat Muffins

Makes 12 muffins

1 cup whole wheat pastry flour

1¼ cup rolled oats

2 teaspoons baking powder

1 teaspoon cinnamon

¼ teaspoon sea salt

½ cup maple syrup

3 tablespoons canola oil

¼ cup applesauce

¼ cup + 1 tablespoon water

egg replacer for 1 egg

2 medium apples, grated

**Preheat** the oven to 375°

**In a large bowl**, combine the flour, oats, baking powder, cinnamon, and salt.

**In a food processor,** combine the maple syrup, oil, applesauce, water, and egg replacer.

**Pour** the liquid ingredients into the dry, and fold until blended, but do not over mix.

**Fold** the apples into the batter. You can leave the skins on the apples if they are organic.

**Line** 12 muffin cups with unbleached paper liners, and fill half way using a ¼ cup ice cream scoop.

**Bake** for 20 minutes until a tooth pick inserted in the center comes out clean.

**Remove** the muffins from the oven, and transfer to a wire rack to cool.

Per muffin: Calories: 148, Protein: 3 gm., Fat: 3 gm., Carbohydrates: 25 gm.

**Variation:** Add ⅓ cup chopped pecans to the batter during mixing. For a streusel topping, combine 1 tablespoon dehydrated cane sugar with ½ teaspoon cinnamon, and sprinkle on top of each muffin before baking.

# Mimi's Molded Cookies

Yield: 20 large cookies

**Cream** the Spectrum Spread with the dehydrated cane juice sweetener.

**Beat** in the egg replacer and soymilk.

**In a separate bowl**, combine the flour, salt, and cinnamon.

**Combine** both mixtures and knead until all the flour is blended.

**Place** on wax paper and roll into a log or a ball. Refrigerate overnight.

**Preheat** the oven to 350°.

**Roll** the dough out on a floured surface, and cut out shapes as desired.

**Place** on a lightly oiled cookie sheet, and bake 10 to 12 minutes.

**Remove** from the oven, transfer to a wire rack, and let cool.

**Ice** and or decorate as desired or top with Tofu Cream Cheese Frosting (page 126).

Per cookie: Calories: 136, Protein: 2 gm., Fat: 5 gm., Carbohydrates: 19 gm.

½ cup Spectrum Spread or canola oil

¾ cup dehydrated cane juice sweetener

egg replacer for 1 egg

1 tablespoon soymilk

3 cups whole wheat pastry flour or white wheat flour

¼ teaspoon sea salt

¼ teaspoon cinnamon or nutmeg

*About this recipe*——

Let the kids use cookie cutters for various occasions such as Halloween, Christmas, Valentine's Day, etc.

# Tofu Cream Cheese Frosting

Yield: about ½ cup

½ cup Tofu Cream Cheese
   (page 34)
⅛ cup maple syrup
½ teaspoon almond extract

**Combine** all ingredients until smooth. Use pureed parsley for green color, and beets or cranberries for red color.

**For the holidays**, you may want to consider making the recipe and dividing it in half. Leave ½ white. Divide the other half, and color ½ green and ½ red.

Per tablespoon: Calories: 64, Protein: 2 gm.,
   Fat: 2 gm., Carbohydrates: 8 gm..

# Cheezy Popcorn

Yield: 6 cups

1 clove garlic, minced
1 teaspoon olive oil
1 teaspoon dried parsley
1 teaspoon dried basil
6 cups popped corn
2 tablespoons nutritional yeast
   or soy parmesan cheese

**In a small saucepan**, sauté the garlic for 2 minutes in the olive oil. Turn off the heat, and add the parsley and basil. Drizzle the mixture over the popcorn. Sprinkle the nutritional yeast on top, and mix.

Per cup: Calories: 45, Protein: 2 gm., Fat: 1 gm.,
   Carbohydrates: 7 gm.

**Variation:** Spray the popcorn with olive oil and season with nutritional yeast, spike, and soy parmesan cheese.

## About this recipe——

One-third cup of uncooked corn will make six to eight cups popped.

# Jam Filled Muffins

**Preheat** the oven to 400°.

**Make** Carrot Raisin Muffins (page 123), your favorite muffin batter recipe, or muffin mix from a box.

**Spoon** the batter into a miniature muffin tin until half full. Place ¼ teaspoon of their favorite jelly on top, and then top with the remaining batter.

**Bake** approximately 12 minutes.

Per serving: Calories: 160, Protein: 3 gm., Fat: 2 gm., Carbohydrates: 33 gm.

*About this recipe* ──

Here's a fun way to increase the chances of your child eating a nutritious muffin.

# Baked Potato Chips

Serves 4

**Slice** the raw potatoes paper thin, and spread out on an oiled cookie sheet.

**Bake** in a 400° oven for 15 or 20 minutes.

**Remove** the potatoes when cooked to a crisp, golden brown. For a fun variation, peel the sweet potatoes with a vegetable peeler and bake.

**You can** also make these in a microwave oven.

**Slice** the potatoes ¹⁄₁₆ inch thick.

**Spray** a microwaveable plate with cooking spray, and lay out the slices so they do not overlap.

Microwave on high for 5 minutes, turn the slices over, and microwave 2 more minutes until they are crisp. Cool in the oven. You can also use this method with carrots, butternut squash, plantains, zucchini, and other vegetables. Serve with your favorite vegetable dip.

4 baking potatoes or sweet potatoes, washed and peeled

*About this recipe* ──

This is an easy way to cook up potatoes and sweet potatoes in a hurry.

Per serving: Calories: 131, Protein: 2 gm., Fat: 0 gm., Carbohydrates: 31 gm.

# Baked Pita Chips

Yield: 36 wedges

3 whole wheat pita breads

**Preheat** the oven to 300°.

**Cut** the pita bread in half crosswise. Pull the halves apart, stack them, and cut in half. Cut each half into three wedges.

**Place** the wedges on an ungreased cookie sheet, and bake for 30 minutes until browned and crisp. Be sure to turn the wedges occasionally. Serve with dips and salads. Try the Mock Guacamole recipe (page 32).

Per wedge: Calories: 14, Protein: 1 gm., Fat: 0 gm., Carbohydrates: 3 gm.

**Variation:** Mix ½ cup soy parmesan cheese, 1½ teaspoons paprika, ½ teaspoon garlic powder, and ½ teaspoon basil. Lightly spray the pita wedges with cooking spray, sprinkle on the soy parmesan cheese mix, and bake.

# Baked Corn Tortilla Chips

6 corn tortillas

**Preheat** the oven to 350°.

**Cut** the tortillas in half, stack the halves, and cut into 3 wedges. Place the tortilla wedges on an ungreased cookie sheet, and bake for 15 to 20 minutes until crispy. Serve with corn salsa. They can also be used in the Taco Ole Salad (page 76).

Per tortilla: Calories: 65, Protein: 2 gm., Fat: 1 gm., Carbohydrates: 12 gm.

**Variation:** Mix ¼ teaspoon cumin, ½ teaspoon chili powder, ⅛ teaspoon sea salt, and ⅛ teaspoon onion powder. Lightly spray the tortilla pieces with cooking spray, sprinkle on the seasoning mix, and bake.

# Joe and Anna's Fruit Salad

Serves 10 to 12

**Scoop** balls out of the melons with a scooper, and place in a large serving bowl.

**Toss** in the grapes and blueberries, and gently mix.

**Add** the strawberries, and garnish the top with the kiwis. Serve chilled or at room temperature.

**Variation:** Cut out the watermelon, leaving a handle across the top to look like a basket, and fill with the fruit salad. You can place flowers around the bottom to decorate.

Per serving: Calories: 107, Protein: 1 gm., Fat: 0 gm., Carbohydrates: 23 gm.

1 watermelon

1 cantaloupe

2 cups green, seedless grapes

2 cups red, seedless grapes

1 pint blueberries

1 pint strawberries, sliced

2 kiwis, peeled and sliced

*Did you know?*

Berries are recommended to help keep the blood from thickening.

# Fruit 'N Vanilla Cookies

Serves 4

2 peaches, cut into wedges

2 cups blueberries

8 vanilla cookies

4 tablespoons orange juice

**Combine** the peaches and blueberries, and pour into 4 serving bowls.

**Garnish** each bowl with 2 cookies, broken up. Pour 1 tablespoon orange juice over each bowl, and serve.

Per serving: Calories: 110, Protein: 1 gm., Fat: 3 gm., Carbohydrates: 21 gm.

# Fruit Medley

Serves 4

4 nectarines, cut up

2 bananas, sliced

1 cup blueberries

1 tablespoon orange juice

1 tablespoon plain rice or
  soymilk

**Combine** the nectarines, bananas, and blueberries in a medium-size bowl. Drizzle with the orange juice and rice milk. Let set for a few minutes in the refrigerator, and serve.

Per serving: Calories: 112, Protein: 1 gm., Fat: 0 gm., Carbohydrates: 26 gm.

## Did you know?

Phytochemicals are compounds found in fruits and vegetables that appear to offer protection from cancer.

# Animal Cookie Fruit Bowl

Serves 4

**Gently mix** the peaches, kiwis, and blueberries in a medium-size serving bowl.

**Pour** the fruit into 4 serving bowls and add ⅛ cup rice milk or soymilk to each bowl. Garnish each fruit bowl with 5 animal cookies.

Per serving: Calories: 177, Protein: 4 gm., Fat: 3 gm., Carbohydrates: 34 gm.

4 peaches, peeled and sliced

4 kiwis, peeled and sliced

1 cup blueberries

½ cup vanilla rice or soymilk

20 animal cookies

### Did you know?

Kiwi fruit is a good source of fiber and Vitamin C. One kiwi fruit provides 75 mg. of Vitamin C.

# Fruit Jello

Serves 4

**Bring** the juice and the agar to a boil, and simmer for 2-3 minutes.

**Pour** into a bowl, and let set for 10 minutes.

**Add** the strawberries. The agar will gel at room temperature in 45 minutes.

**Experiment** with different varieties of fruit, such as peaches, nectarines, kiwi, mandarin orange slices, or pineapple.

Per serving: Calories: 79, Protein: 0 gm., Fat: 0 gm., Carbohydrates: 19 gm.

2 cups apple-strawberry juice

2 tablespoons agar flakes

½ pound fresh strawberries, chopped

### Did you know?

Agar is derived from seaweed and is a natural, vegetarian alternative to gelatin. Gelatin is derived from collagen, the prime constituent of the connective tissue in animals.

# Banana Date Smoothie

Yield: 4 small servings

1 cup orange juice

2 bananas, frozen

3 pitted dates

**Blend** all the ingredients until smooth, and serve immediately, or pour into popsicle molds and freeze.

Per cup: Calories: 98, Protein: 1 gm., Fat: 0 gm., Carbohydrates: 23 gm.

## Did you know?

Be sure to drink enough water every day. Eight glasses of water are recommended for the average person per day. Those who are physically active need more. If you work out, drink 8 to 20 oz. of water 15 minutes before working out. If you jog for fun, drink at least 2 cups for every pound you lose on your run.

# Pineapple Banana Smoothie

Yield: 2 cups

1 cup orange juice

1 cup pineapple juice

2 bananas, frozen

1 date, pitted

**Blend** all the ingredients until smooth, and drink or put into popsicle molds, and freeze. It's a great treat for kids.

Per cup: Calories: 242, Protein: 2 gm., Fat: 0 gm., Carbohydrates: 56 gm.

## Did you know?

Bananas have large amounts of potassium, a mineral necessary for regulating the heartbeat and the body's balance of sodium. One banana contains 450 mg. of potassium.

# Sweet Tooth Desserts

# Sasha's Oatmeal Raisin Cookies

Yield: 26 cookies

1½ cups rolled oats

⅔ cup + 2 tablespoons whole wheat pastry flour

½ teaspoon baking soda

½ teaspoon sea salt

¼ cup canola oil or Spectrum spread

¼ cup applesauce

⅓-½ cup maple syrup

½ cup raisins, soaked in water for 10 minutes and drained

**Preheat** the oven to 325°.

**Mix** the oats, flour, baking soda, salt, oil, applesauce, maple syrup, and raisins in a medium-size bowl.

**Oil** a baking sheet with canola spray, and use a tablespoon to spoon out each cookie.

**Bake** for 15 minutes.

Per cookie: Calories: 71, Protein: 1 gm., Fat: 2 gm., Carbohydrates: 11 gm.

**Variation:** Add ½ cup walnuts, pecans, or sunflower seeds, or dairy free chocolate chips or carob chips.

Per cookie: Calories: 85, Protein: 2 gm., Fat: 4 gm., Carbohydrates: 11 gm.

## Did you know?

Dried fruits are a good source of iron and provide a concentrated source of energy. They should always be soaked before eating

# Low-Fat Chocolate Chip Cookies

Yield: 28 cookies

**Preheat** the oven to 350°.

**In a large mixing bowl**, combine the flours, dehydrated cane juice sweetener, and baking soda.

**In a food processor** or blender, combine the Prune Puree, maple syrup, vanilla, and water.

**Combine** the wet and dry ingredients in a large mixing bowl, and add the chocolate chips and nuts.

**Lightly spray** a cookie sheet with oil. Drop level tablespoons of dough onto the cookie sheet, about 1 inch apart.

**Bake** for 10 to 12 minutes. Remove from the oven, and transfer to a wire rack to cool.

Per cookie: Calories: 77, Protein: 2 gm., Fat: 1 gm., Carbohydrates: 15 gm.

2 cups white wheat flour or whole wheat pastry flour

½ cup rolled oat flour

⅔ cup dehydrated cane juice sweetener

¾ teaspoon baking soda

¼ cup Prune Puree (page 136)

2 tablespoons maple syrup

1 teaspoon vanilla

¼ cup water

½ cup non-dairy chocolate chips or carob chips (optional)

½ cup chopped walnuts (optional)

# Prune Puree

Yield: 1 cup

1½ cups pitted prunes
6 tablespoons water

**Place** the prunes and water in a blender, and pulse until the prunes are well chopped.

Per tablespoon: Calories: 36, Protein: 0 gm.,
Fat: 0 gm., Carbohydrates: 9 gm.

## Did you know?

Many food manufacturers are are using prune puree as an alternative to butter in baked goods. You can substitute an equal amount of prune puree for butter, margarine, or oil. This can help cut the fat in recipes by 75% to 90%, and reduce the calories by 20% to 30%.

# Cheyenne's Carob Chip Cookies

Yield: 30 cookies

**Preheat** the oven to 350°.

**In a large mixing bowl**, combine the flour, oats, salt, and baking soda.

**Stir** in the walnuts, apricots, and carob chips.

**In a blender** or food processor, blend together the maple syrup, oil, applesauce, vanilla, and water.

**Pour** the liquid into the dry ingredients, and mix to a thick batter. Drop by 1 tablespoon measure onto an oiled cookie sheet about 1 inch apart, and bake 12 to 15 minutes. When cooked, transfer to a cooling rack.

Per cookie: Calories: 94, Protein: 2 gm., Fat: 5 gm., Carbohydrates: 11 gm.

2 cups whole wheat pastry flour

½ cup rolled oats

½ teaspoon sea salt

¼ teaspoon baking soda

¾ cup walnuts, coarsely chopped

½ cup dried apricots, coarsely chopped (optional)

¾ cup carob or dairy-free chocolate chips chips

½ cup maple syrup

¼ cup canola oil

¼ cup applesauce

1 teaspoon vanilla

3-4 tablespoons water or juice

## Did you know?

Carob is often recommended for hypoglycemic adults and hyperactive children because it contains no harmful stimulants.

# Carob Almond Macaroons

Yield: 15 macaroons

7½ oz. low-fat carob soymilk

1 tablespoon carob powder

½ tablespoon coffee substitute

1½ tablespoons maple syrup

½ teaspoon vanilla

¼ cup currants, soaked in
water for 10 minutes and
drained

1 cup + 2 tablespoons
unsweetened, shredded
coconut

¼ cup almonds, chopped

⅓ cup whole wheat pastry flour

¼ teaspoon sea salt

**Combine** the soymilk and carob in a small saucepan.

**Place** the saucepan in a small skillet filled with water, and bring to a boil. Stir the mixture with a wire whisk for 5 minutes over boiling water.

**Remove** from the burner and add the coffee substitute, maple syrup, and vanilla.

**In a small mixing bowl**, mix the currants, coconut, almonds, flour, and salt.

**Preheat** the oven to 350°.

**Pour** the milk mixture in with the currant mixture, and mix well. Drop by ⅛ cupfuls onto an oiled cookie sheet, and bake for 10 minutes. Set on a rack to cool.

Per macaroon: Calories: 157, Protein: 2 gm.,
Fat: 11 gm., Carbohydrates: 10 gm.

## Did you know?

It takes 16 pounds of grain and soy to produce one pound of beef.

# Mimi's Brown Rice Crispies

Yield: 16 squares

**Dry roast** the almonds in a small saucepan, set aside to cool, and chop.

**Mix** together the peanut butter, nutmeg, rice syrup, allspice, and cinnamon in a medium saucepan on low heat, stirring continuously.

**Add** the almonds and apricots to the heated mixture. Mix well and remove from the heat.

**Add** the vanilla and cereal, and mix well together.

**Spread** the mixture in an oiled 8-inch square pan. It will spread more easily if your fingers are damp.

**Place** in the refrigerator to chill. Cut into 16 squares.

¼ cup almonds

1½ tablespoons peanut butter

¼ teaspoon nutmeg

½ cup brown rice syrup

⅛ teaspoon allspice

½ teaspoon cinnamon

¼ cup apricots, chopped

1 teaspoon vanilla

3 cups brown rice crispy cereal

Per square: Calories: 77, Protein: 1 gm., Fat: 1 gm., Carbohydrates: 14 gm.

**Serving Suggestion:** Purchase a teddy bear mold at a cake and candy supply or crafts store. Lightly oil the mold and press the cereal mixture into the mold, being sure to press firmly into crevices. Place waxed paper over the mold, invert, and pop out. Decorate using whole cloves for eyes and buttons. Tie a narrow ribbon into a bow around the neck.

# Maple Almond Squares

Yield: 24 large squares

1 cup almonds

1 cup currants, soaked in water
   for 10 minutes and drained

2 cups whole wheat pastry flour

½ cup dehydrated cane juice
   sweetener or date sugar

1½ teaspoons baking powder

¼ teaspoon baking soda

¼ teaspoon sea salt

¼ cup safflower or canola oil

1 teaspoon egg replacer mixed
   with 1 tablespoon water

¼ cup maple syrup

½ cup plain soymilk

1 teaspoon vanilla

**Place** the almonds in a blender, and chop for 10 seconds. Set in a small mixing bowl.

**Add** the currants to the almonds, and set aside.

**Preheat** the oven to 350°.

**Combine** the flour, dehydrated cane juice sweetener, baking powder, baking soda, and salt in a large mixing bowl, and mix well.

**Pour** the oil, egg replacer mix, and maple syrup into the flour mixture, and stir well.

**Add** the soymilk and vanilla to the batter.

**Stir** in the almonds and the currants until well blended.

**Spread** onto an oiled 13 x 9½ x 2-inch pan, and bake for 20 minutes. Let cool before cutting.

Per square: Calories: 151, Protein: 3 gm., Fat: 5 gm., Carbohydrates: 23 gm.

# Strawberry Kiwi Fruit Tart

## Serves 12

**Preheat** the oven to 375°.

**Using an electric blender** or coffee grinder, grind up the graham crackers.

**In a small bowl**, combine the graham cracker crumbs with the oil, water, cinnamon, and maple syrup, and mix well.

**Press** the mixture into an oiled 10-inch tart pan or pie plate, and bake for 7 minutes. Remove and cool.

**In a small saucepan**, sprinkle the agar flakes over the water and pineapple juice, and let set for one minute. Bring to a simmer over medium heat, cook for 2 minutes without stirring, and set aside.

**Blend** the vanilla soy yogurt, soy sour cream, rice milk, lemon juice, and maple syrup in a blender or a food processor.

**Turn** the blender on again, and slowly add the agar-pineapple mixture through the feed cap. Continue blending until smooth.

**Pour** the blended mixture into the graham cracker crust. Cover, refrigerate, and chill for at least 3 hours before serving until firm.

**Just before serving**, arrange the sliced strawberries along the edge of the tart. Next, place the blueberries in a circle along the inside edge of the strawberries. Over-lap the kiwi slices and arrange alongside the blueberries. Complete the design with a few strawberry slices placed like a petal in the center of the tart.

2 cups graham crackers

⅛ cup canola oil

⅛ cup water

1 teaspoon cinnamon

½ tablespoon maple syrup

4 tablespoons agar flakes

½ cup cold water

¾ cup pineapple juice, unsweetened

1 cup vanilla soy yogurt

½ cup soy sour cream

½ cup plain rice milk or soymilk

1 teaspoon lemon juice

2-3 tablespoons maple syrup

2 cups strawberries, sliced

½-1 cup blueberries

2 kiwi fruits, peeled and sliced

Per serving: Calories: 107, Protein: 2 gm., Fat: 4 gm., Carbohydrates: 14 gm.

# Carob Pudding

Serves 4

5 tablespoons arrowroot

2 cups carob or plain lite
 soymilk

2 tablespoons carob powder

¼ cup maple syrup

¼ teaspoon grain coffee
 substitute (optional)

**In a small bowl**, combine the arrowroot and ¼ cup of the soymilk, and dissolve thoroughly.

**Place** the rest of the soymilk in a medium-size pot, and add the arrowroot mixture, carob powder, maple syrup, and coffee substitute.

**Cook over medium heat**, stirring constantly, until thickened. Place in a bowl and refrigerate. Chill and serve.

Per serving: Calories: 145, Protein: 2 gm., Fat: 1 gm.,
 Carbohydrates: 32 gm.

## Did you know?

Chocolate, nicotine, and caffeine are believed to stimulate the development of breast tumors.

# Vanilla Pudding

Serves 4

5 tablespoons arrowroot

2 cups vanilla soymilk

⅛ cup maple syrup

1 teaspoon vanilla

**In a small bowl**, combine the arrowroot and ¼ cup of the soymilk, and dissolve thoroughly.

**In a medium-size saucepan**, heat the soymilk, adding the arrowroot and stirring constantly until thickened. **Bring** to a low boil until thickened. Lower the heat, cover, and cook about 15 minutes.

**Remove** from the heat, add the maple syrup and vanilla, and let cool. Refrigerate and serve chilled.

Per serving: Calories: 118, Protein: 4 gm., Fat: 3 gm.,
 Carbohydrates: 19 gm.

**Variation:** Layer the pudding in a parfait glass with Banana Dip (page 155) and granola.

# Banana Bread

Makes 1 loaf (16 slices)

**Preheat** the oven to 350°.

**In a large mixing bowl**, mix together the flour, baking powder, baking soda, salt, and sweetener.

**Mix** the vanilla with the bananas, and place in the center of the mixing bowl. Add the egg replacer mix and applesauce, and mix well.

**Fold** in the walnuts.

**Place** in a well oiled loaf pan, and bake for 50 minutes. Test at about 40 minutes to see if it is done. Insert a toothpick and if it comes out clean, the bread is done. This batter can also be made into banana muffins.

Per slice: Calories: 119, Protein: 2 gm., Fat: 1 gm., Carbohydrates: 24 gm.

**Variation:** Omit the walnuts for a fat-free muffin. Add ¼ cup chopped apricots, if desired.

**Variation:** Replace ¼ cup flour with ¼ cup wheat germ.

2 cups white wheat flour

1 teaspoon baking powder

1 teaspoon baking soda

½ teaspoon sea salt

¾ cup dehydrated cane juice sweetener

1 teaspoon vanilla

1½ cups bananas, mashed

3 teaspoons egg replacer + ¼ cup water

¼ cup applesauce

¼ cup chopped walnuts

# Crumble Topping

Yield: 1½ cups

1 cup whole wheat pastry flour
½ cup pecans, chopped
⅛ cup canola oil
⅛ cup water
pinch of sea salt

**Preheat** the oven to 350°.

**Combine** all the ingredients in a medium-size mixing bowl.

**Spread** the mixture into an oiled 9 x 13-inch pan, and bake for 15 minutes. Cool and use as a topping in parfait, on top of dairy-less yogurt, pudding, and fruit crisp.

Per 2 tablespoons: Calories: 85, Protein: 2 gm., Fat: 4 gm., Carbohydrates: 8 gm.

# Tofu Whipped Cream

Yield: 1½ cups

½ pound soft tofu, well
    drained
⅛ cup canola oil
⅛ cup water
2 tablespoons honey or rice
    syrup
2 tablespoons lemon juice
1 teaspoon vanilla
pinch of sea salt

**Blend** all the ingredients in a blender or food processor, and chill until ready to use. Use as a topping on pudding, fruit jello, and pudding parfait.

Per ½ cup: Calories: 172, Protein: 5 gm., Fat: 11 gm., Carbohydrates: 14 gm.

# Feeding Your Kids Right

"Dear Child, " she chuckled, "When I see

A princess who won't eat a pea

I try to help, for that is my mission

I'm the Delicious Witch of Good Nutrition."

—Karen Greene, *Once Upon A Recipe*

One day I found two pumpkin seeds;

I planted one and pulled the weeds.

It sprouted roots and a big, long vine.

A pumpkin grew; I called it mine.

The pumpkin was quite round and fat.

(I really am quite proud of that.)

But there is something I'll admit

That has me worried quite a bit:

I ate the other seed, you see.

Now will it grow inside of me?

(I'm so relieved since I have found

That pumpkins only grow in the ground!)

(*Sesame Street Magazine,* November 1994)

What vegetable does a pumpkin turn into when an elephant steps on it?"

Squash.

When asked how he was, what did the pumpkin say?

"I'm vine, thank you."

# Feeding Your Kids Right

From the moment of conception, it is a major responsibility to feed your children a nutritionally sound diet. Aveline Kushi, a macrobiotic educator who teaches in the United States and abroad, feels so strongly about this that she believes the cook in the family lays the foundation for the destiny and well-being of his or her offspring and family.

The fast-paced, high-stress world that we live in encourages poor eating habits, cutting corners, and eating on the run. There is a heavy emphasis on overly processed food, fast food, and junk food. Even most of our school lunch programs leave a lot to be desired with their emphasis on high-fat, high-cholesterol meat and dairy foods, and foods with a high sugar content.

Current research studies indicate that one out of every four children in the United States has a cholesterol level that is too high. One in eight children has a cholesterol level that poses a health risk. It is now recommended that, by age two, parents begin to watch their children's diet. According to the American Academy of Pediatrics, children over the age of two can eat a low-fat diet similar to that recommended for adults. This means no more than 30% of your children's calories should come from fat.

Remember, you control what foods are purchased and eaten at home. Make your home and kitchen a place where good habits and attitudes begin. As your child acquires a taste for more nutritious, healthful foods, they will have less desire for sweet, high-fat foods. Encourage your family to make nutritionally sound choices by offering delicious, nutritious, fun foods in the home and to begin their journey into a future of well-being and good health.

# Fun Snack Ideas

How about appealing to your kids on a visual level with food? What better way to get your kids (especially the younger ones) excited about food and cooking, and to slip in some nutritious fruits and vegetables, than to let them put together some fun and creative snacks. Here are some interesting food ideas for kids to create with you.

**Funny Dip Faces**

Place your child's favorite dip in a bowl and decorate.

Clown

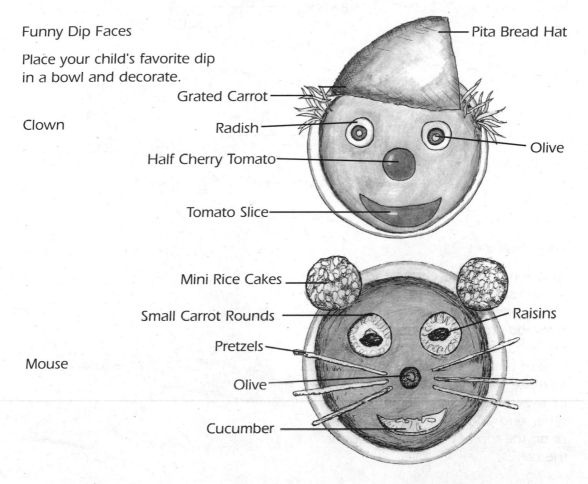

Pita Bread Hat

Grated Carrot

Radish

Olive

Half Cherry Tomato

Tomato Slice

Mouse

Mini Rice Cakes

Small Carrot Rounds

Raisins

Pretzels

Olive

Cucumber

## Yummy Fruit Yogurt Faces

Place your child's favorite soy yogurt in a bowl and decorate.

### Kitty Cat

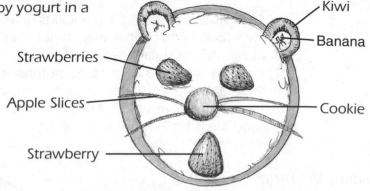

Kiwi

Banana

Strawberries

Apple Slices — Cookie

Strawberry

### Teddy Bear

Oatmeal Cookies

Strawberry Slices

Kiwi Slices — Raisins

Apple Slices — Grape

Kiwi Slice

## Food Airplanes

Take long carrots, clean, and peel. Make a slice lengthwise through the carrot beginning ½ inch from one side and stopping ½ inch from the other side. Slide a thin piece of soy cheese through the slit in the carrot to make the wings. Leave one end of the carrot pointed, and cut the other end and use the cut piece to sit on the top of the pointed end for the tail.

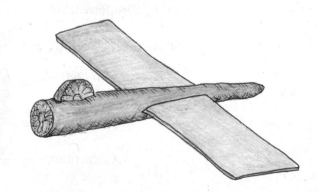

## Food Choo Choo Trains

Make the railroad tracks out of slices of spinach noodles. Broccoli with stems makes great trees to set around the tracks.

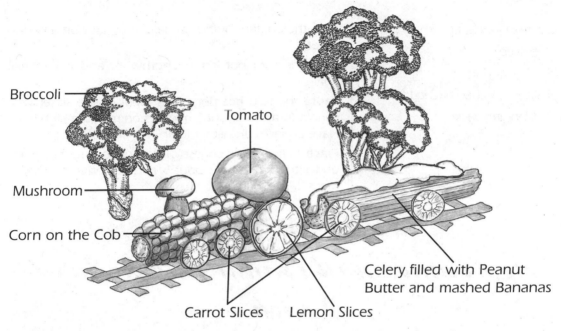

Broccoli

Tomato

Mushroom

Corn on the Cob

Celery filled with Peanut Butter and mashed Bananas

Carrot Slices    Lemon Slices

## Edible Halloween Witch

This is a fun one for kids to make as a special, nutritious Halloween treat.

Freeze full, round scoops of mint flavored rice or soy ice cream on a cookie sheet that can fit in the freezer. (You want the green for a creepy color.) Cut natural licorice into long strands for the hair and mouth. Use a cashew nut for a crooked nose. Use raisins for eyes. Place a natural whole grain ice cream cone on top of the witches head for a hat. The kids can make them and eat them, or refreeze them to serve later.

# Little Tyke's Lunches
## Open Face Cheese Melts

Yield: 4 sandwiches

2 whole wheat English muffins, halved

4 tofu hot dogs

4 slices soy cheese (cheddar or Monterey Jack)

**Slice** the English muffins in half, and place on a baking sheet.

**Slice** the tofu hot dogs lengthwise, and cut in half again.

**Sauté** the tofu hot dogs in a medium-size skillet with canola spray for about 2 minutes on medium-high heat. Place 2 pieces on each muffin.

**Place** 1 slice of the cheese on top of each muffin. Place under the broiler for about 5 minutes until the cheese melts. Serve warm.

Per sandwich: Calories: 156, Protein: 11 gm., Fat: 4 gm., Carbohydrates: 17 gm.

# Applesauce and Peanut Butter Sandwich

Yield: 4 sandwiches

8 slices whole grain bread

2 tablespoons peanut butter per slice

2 tablespoons sugar-free apple-sauce per slice

**Remove** the crust from the bread.

**Spread** the peanut butter on 4 of the slices.

**Spread** the applesauce on the other 4 slices. Place the halves together, and cut into quarters.

Per sandwich: Calories: 341, Protein: 13 gm., Fat: 17 gm., Carbohydrates: 34 gm.

## Food for thought . . .

"Healthy soil makes healthy plants, healthy plants make healthy food, healthy food leads to healthy people," Judy Brown.

# Crinkle Carrot Fries

Serves 4

**Use** a french fry cutter to cut the carrots into a french fry shape.

**Place** the carrots in a steamer, and steam for about 10 minutes until crisp tender. Season with soy parmesan cheese if desired.

Per serving: Calories: 31, Protein: 1 gm., Fat: 0 gm., Carbohydrates: 7 gm.

4 carrots

# Fruit Kabobs

Serves 8 (16 6-inch kabobs)

**Alternate** the pieces of the pineapple, grapes, strawberries, and melon on wooden skewers. Each kabob should have 2 of each fruit. In a separate container, provide vanilla soy yogurt as a dipping sauce.

Per serving: Calories: 66, Protein: 1 gm., Fat: 0 gm., Carbohydrates: 14 gm.

**Variation:** You can also use star fruit or papaya. For a yogurt and cream cheese dip, mix together ½ cup vanilla soy yogurt, ¼ cup Tofu Cream Cheese (page 34), ½ tablespoon maple syrup or 1 tablespoon rice syrup, and ¼ teaspoon cinnamon. For a strawberry dip, blend fresh strawberries with a little maple syrup.

1 (12 oz.) can pineapple chunks, drained

½ cup green or red seedless grapes

1 pint whole strawberries, tops removed

½ cantaloupe or honeydew melon, cut in large chunks

*About this recipe*——

You can use these kabobs as a centerpiece. Stick the kabobs into the outside skin of a pineapple or melon half, and arrange 4 snow peas on the top of each skewer like the leaves on a palm tree.

# Vegetable Kabobs

Serves 4 (8 6-inch kabobs)

1 cucumber, peeled, cut in half, and sliced

½ red, yellow, or green peppers, cut in 16 chunks

16 whole cherry tomatoes

16 whole mushrooms

soy cheese (optional)

**Alternate** the pieces of cucumber, red, peppers, cherry tomatoes, and mushrooms on a skewer. If desired, you can add chunks of soy cheese.

**In a separate container**, provide a dip made from plain soy yogurt mixed with your favorite herbal seasoning.

Per serving: Calories: 36, Protein: 1 gm., Fat: 0 gm., Carbohydrates: 7 gm.

# Sandwich Kabobs

Serves 4 (4 6-inch kabobs)

½ cup carrots, grated

½ recipe Tofu Cream Cheese (page 34) or Cashew Cheese (page 35)

4 slices whole grain bread

soy cheese, cut in chunks (optional)

**Mix** the grated carrots with the Tofu Cream Cheese (page 34).

**Make** sandwiches with the whole grain bread, carrots, and cream cheese filling, and cut the sandwiches into bite size cubes.

**Alternately arrange** the sandwich cubes and chopped vegetables (refer to Vegetable Kabobs) on a skewer. Chunks of soy cheese can also be added. Serve with your favorite dip.

Per serving: Calories: ,132 Protein: 6 gm., Fat: 4 gm., Carbohydrates: 16 gm.

*About this recipe*——

Kabobs are a fun food to pack up and can be made with a wide variety of foods.

# Kate's Favorite Baked Fries

Serves 4 to 6

**Cut** up the potatoes with a french fry cutter for a real french fry shape.

**Preheat** the oven to 350°.

**Place** the soy parmesan cheese, garlic, and parsley in a large baggie.

**Place** a handful of potatoes in the bag at a time, and shake to coat them well.

**Put** the coated potatoes on an oiled baking sheet, and bake for 30 minutes or until golden brown.

Per serving: Calories: 157, Protein: 4 gm., Fat: 1 gm., Carbohydrates: 33 gm.

6 baking potatoes, scrubbed and peeled

¼ cup soy parmesan cheese

1 teaspoon garlic powder

1 tablespoon dried parsley

# Veggie Schooner Sandwiches

Yield: 4 sandwiches

**Mix** the Mock Chicken Salad, apple, sunflower seeds, and extra soy mayonnaise if it is too dry.

**Spread** the salad on top of the English muffin halves. To make the sails for the schooner place 2 tortilla chips straight on top of the salad.

Per sandwich: Calories: 238, Protein: 24 gm., Fat: 3 gm., Carbohydrates: 25 gm.

1 recipe Mock Chicken Salad (page 38) or Tempeh Salad (page 37)

½ cup apple, chopped

1 tablespoon sunflower seeds

4 whole wheat English muffin halves

tortilla chips

# Dip Suggestions

## Spinach Dip

1 (10 oz.) package frozen
   chopped spinach, thawed
   and drained
2 cups plain soy yogurt
½ cup green onions, chopped
½ teaspoon sea salt
¼ teaspoon pepper

**Mix** all the ingredients.

Per 2 tablespoons: Calories: 23, Protein: 1 gm.,
   Fat: 0 gm., Carbohydrates: 2 gm.

## Fruit Dip

1 cup plain soy yogurt
¼ cup apricot preserves

Per 2 tablespoons: Calories: 44, Protein: 1 gm.,
   Fat: 1 gm., Carbohydrates: 7 gm.

## Curry Dip

½ cup tofu mayonnaise
½ cup soy sour cream
honey mustard to taste
curry powder to taste

Per 2 tablespoons: Calories: 49, Protein: 1 gm.,
   Fat: 3 gm., Carbohydrates: 2 gm.

## Yogurt Dip

1 cup plain soy yogurt
¼ cup tofu mayonnaise
1 teaspoon lemon juice

Per 2 tablespoons: Calories: 37, Protein: 1 gm.,
   Fat: 2 gm., Carbohydrates: 2 gm.

**Variation:** For an herbed variation, season with garlic, basil,
dill weed, onion flakes, sun-dried tomatoes, oregano, etc.

## Banana Dip

Yield: 1 cup

½ cup soft tofu, drained

1 tablespoon lemon juice

3 bananas

2 tablespoons maple syrup

1 teaspoon vanilla

**In a blender** or food processor, blend all the ingredients together. Use as a dipping sauce for fruit skewers and frozen fruit snacks. Use as a layering ingredient in parfait glasses with puddings, or serve a dollop on carob or chocolate pudding.

Per ½ cup: Calories: 257, Protein: 6 gm., Fat: 4 gm., Carbohydrates: 50 gm.

## About these recipes——

Here are some low fat dipper suggestions to use instead of fried corn or potato chips:

* carrots, celery, red, yellow, or green peppers, zucchini, broccoli, cauliflower, cherry tomatoes

* pretzels, whole grain crackers, matzos, rice cakes

*apples, pears, melon balls, strawberries, peaches, nectarine

## Did you know?

Bernard Jensen recommends children eat a raw carrot before each meal. He believes this strengthens the lower jaw and helps to straighten out their teeth. Don't throw away the tops either. They are full of potassium. Paul Pitchford, author of Healing with Whole Foods, says, "Eating carrot sticks daily helps strengthen children's teeth and, in some cases, reduces overcrowding of the teeth by encouraging the development of the lower jaw."

# Tofu Meatballs

Yield: 12 to 13 non-meatballs

1 pound extra firm tofu, mashed

½ cup corn flakes, crushed

¼ cup oats

2 tablespoons soy sauce

½ cup onion, chopped

½ tablespoon peanut butter

**Preheat** the oven to 400°.

**Mix** all the ingredients together in a medium-size mixing bowl.

**Measure** ¼ cup mixture per meatball. Roll into a ball with your hands. Place the balls on an oiled cookie sheet, and bake for 20 minutes. Serve on top of Quick and Easy Spaghetti Sauce (page 156) and angel hair pasta.

**Variation:** You can roll the meatballs in whole wheat flour before baking.

Per tofu meatball: Calories: 48, Protein: 4 gm., Fat: 2 gm., Carbohydrates: 4 gm.

# Quick and Easy Spaghetti Sauce

Serves 4

1 cup broccoli, chopped

1 can tomato sauce

1 cup roasted red peppers, chopped

**Steam** the broccoli for 5 minutes.

**In a medium saucepan**, mix together the tomato sauce, red peppers, and broccoli, and heat for 5 minutes on medium heat until warmed. Serve on angel hair pasta. Sprinkle with soy parmesan cheese and Tofu Meatballs (page 156).

Per serving (sauce only): Calories: 214, Protein: 8 gm., Fat: 0 gm., Carbohydrates: 43 gm.

## Did you know?

The Journal of the American Cancer Institute (Dec. 6, 1995) published a study which found that lycopene, a carotenoid found in tomatoes and tomato products such as tomato sauce and juice, was shown to reduce the risk of prostate cancer by 45%.

# Anna's Broccoli Slaw

Serves 8

**Using** a food processor, separately chop the broccoli, carrots, and onion to a fine consistency.

**Mix** all the vegetables together in a medium-size mixing bowl.

**In a small bowl**, prepare the dressing by stirring together the mayonnaise, rice vinegar, brown rice syrup, and celery seed.

**Combine** the dressing with the chopped vegetables. Chill for several hours or overnight.

Per serving: Calories: 65, Protein: 1 gm., Fat: 3 gm., Carbohydrates: 7 gm.

1 head broccoli

2 carrots

1 small onion

½ cup tofu mayonnaise

1 tablespoon brown rice or balsamic vinegar

2 teaspoons brown rice syrup or honey

1 teaspoon celery seed

# Waldorf Salad

Serves 6

**Mix** all the ingredients together, and chill.

Per serving: Calories: 133, Protein: 1 gm., Fat: 5 gm., Carbohydrates: 19 gm.

3 large apples, chopped

1 cup celery, chopped

¼ cup walnuts, chopped

¼ cup raisins, or ½ cup seedless red grapes, cut in half

⅓ cup tofu mayonnaise

1 tablespoon brown rice syrup or honey

2 kiwi fruit, peeled, halved lengthwise, and sliced (optional)

## Did you know?

Apples contain 50% more vitamin A than oranges. They are rich in vitamin C which helps to keep bones and teeth strong. They are good blood purifiers. Apples also contain a good amount of calcium. You can make a tea that is beneficial for the kidneys by steeping apple peels.

Grapes are a good source of boron, a mineral believed to be important in maintaining and building healthy bones.

# Banana Logs

Serves 1

1 banana, peeled

1 tablespoon lemon juice

1 tablespoon maple syrup

1 tablespoon chopped coconut

1 tablespoon crushed nuts
   (optional)

**Roll** the whole bananas in the lemon juice and maple syrup.

**Roll** in the coconut or crushed nuts. Serve chilled. You can also freeze these.

Per banana: Calories: 267, Protein: 3 gm., Fat: 13 gm., Carbohydrates: 33 gm.

# Strawberry Jam

Yield: 1 cup

2 cups bananas

2 cups strawberries

1 teaspoon lemon juice

**Blend** all the ingredients together until smooth, and simmer in a small saucepan until thickened.

Per 2 tablespoons: Calories: 46, Protein: 1 gm., Fat: 0 gm., Carbohydrates: 10 gm.

## About this recipe——

This is a great jam for muffins or peanut butter and jelly sandwiches.

# Frozen Carob-Dipped Bananas

Serves 4

**To make a carob syrup**, combine the rice milk, carob powder, almond butter, and maple syrup in a blender.

**Pour** the syrup into a small saucepan, and turn the heat on medium.

**In a cup**, mix the arrowroot and water.

**Add** to the carob syrup, and stir until thick, about 10 minutes. This makes about 1 cup syrup. Refrigerate until ready to use.

**Cover** a baking sheet with wax paper, and lightly spray with canola spray.

**Pour** about ¼ cup of the carob syrup on a plate or in a container large enough to hold the entire banana. Roll the banana in the syrup to cover, and place single file on the waxed paper. On areas where the banana didn't get coated with the syrup, lightly pour more syrup over the banana. Sprinkle the chopped walnuts over the top of each banana.

**Place** in the freezer and allow to freeze for 1 hour. Cover with waxed paper and continue freezing at least 3 hours or longer until the banana is frozen through. The bananas can be eaten whole or cut into slices and served along or with non-dairy vanilla ice cream.

Per serving: Calories: 379, Protein: 5 gm., Fat: 15 gm., Carbohydrates: 53 gm.

**Variation:** For a quick dipped banana, cut the banana in half, spread with vanilla soy yogurt, and roll in crushed graham crackers or cookie crumbs. Push a stick into the end, and eat as is or freeze.

½ cup plain or vanilla, rice milk or lite soymilk

¼ cup + 2 tablespoons carob powder

3 tablespoons almond butter

4 tablespoons maple syrup

1 teaspoon arrowroot powder

1 teaspoon water

4 bananas, peeled

½ cup walnuts, chopped

## Did you know?

Arrowroot was named by the South American Indians who use it to heal poison arrow wounds. Arrowroot is a substitute for cornstarch and is nutritionally superior to cornstarch.

# Birthday Party Lunch
## Party Punch

Serves 12

2 bottles chilled
   apple-strawberry juice
1 bottle chilled nonalcoholic
   sparkling apple juice
ice cubes
strawberries for garnish

**In a large punch bowl**, mix together the apple-strawberry juice and the sparkling apple juice. Add the ice cubes to keep cold, and garnish with whole strawberries.

Per serving: Calories: 149, Protein: 0 gm., Fat: 0 gm., Carbohydrates: 37 gm.

## Lemon-Orange Juice

Serves 4

¼ cup lemon juice
32 oz. orange juice
4 lemon wedges

**Blend** the lemon and orange juice.
**Serve** each 8 oz glass with a wedge of fresh lemon.

Per serving: Calories: 116, Protein: 1 gm., Fat: 0 gm., Carbohydrates: 27 gm.

## Bear Faced Mini Pizzas

**Begin** with whole wheat English muffins or 6-inch whole wheat pita rounds. Cover the top with pasta sauce, leaving 1 inch around the edges. Use thinly sliced potatoes or jerusalem artichokes for the large part of the eye. Use round cucumber slices or carrots for the ears. Use a thinly sliced carrot cut on the diagonal to put inside the eye, and top with a slice of olive. Cut the nose, whiskers, and mouth out of peppers. Bake at 350° for 15 minutes until heated through.

Per serving: Calories: , Protein:  gm., Fat:  gm., Carbohydrates:  gm.

# Banana Boats

Serves 4

**Preheat** the oven to 400°.

**Clean** the bananas thoroughly, leaving the skin on, and wipe dry. Cut the bananas in half lengthwise, leaving the skin intact.

**Place** them in a baking dish facing up. Brush the banana halves with lemon juice to keep from browning, and bake for 10 minutes.

**Place** the baked bananas on 4 serving plates. Scoop 4 melon size balls of vanilla soy ice cream for each banana, and place on top of the bananas. Garnish with the strawberries, or blueberries, or sprinkle on chocolate or carob chips or pieces of a favorite natural candy bar. You can get the little paper party umbrellas or other decorations from the party store to decorate for a special occasion.

2 ripe bananas

2 tablespoons lemon juice

1 cup vanilla soy or rice ice cream

strawberries, blueberries, or chocolate or carob chips

Per serving: Calories: 146, Protein: 1 gm., Fat: 4 gm., Carbohydrates: 26 gm.

# Maple Birthday Cake

Serves 16 to 20

1⅞ cups white wheat flour or
  whole wheat pastry flour

2¼ teaspoons baking powder

2¼ teaspoons baking soda

1 teaspoon sea salt

½ cup canola oil

¼ cup applesauce

1¾ cups maple syrup

1½ cups water

3 tablespoons vanilla

2¼ tablespoons apple cider
  vinegar

**Preheat** the oven to 375°.

**In a large mixing bowl**, mix together the flour, baking powder, baking soda, and salt.

**In a medium size bowl**, whisk together the oil, apple sauce, maple syrup, water, vanilla, and apple cider vinegar.

**Mix** the wet ingredients into the dry.

**Pour** the batter into an oiled 9 x 13-inch baking pan, and bake for 30 to 40 minutes until done.

**Cover** with your favorite icing. I use a Vermont maple icing sold in natural foods stores. For a simple white icing, you can cover with Tofu Cream Cheese (page 34).

Per serving: Calories: 175, Protein: 1 gm., Fat: 6 gm., Carbohydrates: 29 gm.

# Natural Play Clay Recipe

**In a saucepan**, stir together the baking soda and arrowroot. Add the water, and mix well.

**Cook** over medium heat, stirring constantly, until the mixture is the consistency of moist mashed potatoes.

**Turn** out on a plate, and cover with damp cloth until cool enough to handle. Roll to ¼-inch thickness.

**Cut** shapes with cookie cutters. Press a hole near the top of each ornament with a toothpick.

**Allow** the ornaments to dry on a flat surface and harden overnight. Paint, decorate, and protect with a shiny glaze.

2 cups baking soda

1 cup arrowroot

1¼ cups water

# Power Lunches

## Mother Earth's Veggie Special

Serves 4 to 6

1 head broccoli, finely chopped

½ head cauliflower, finely
  chopped

½ red cabbage, thinly shredded

4 celery stalks, diced

4 carrots, shredded

¼ cup tofu mayonnaise or
  favorite mustard (optional)

4 whole grain pita breads, cut
  in half

1 cup soy cheese, grated
  (optional)

**Chop** the vegetables by hand or in a food processor.

**Spread** about 1 tablespoon tofu mayonnaise on the insides of the pita bread.

**Stuff** the pita pocket with the vegetables.

**Add** the soy cheese.

**Serve** with Mother Earth's Essential Dressing (page 165).

**Store** the extra veggies for salads or stir frys and more Veggie Specials during the week.

Per serving (without dressing): Calories: 210,
      Protein: 8 gm., Fat: 0 gm., Carbohydrates: 44 gm.

### About this recipe—

Here's an antioxidant special.

### Did you know?

Cruciferous vegetables, such as broccoli, cabbage, and cauliflower, are high in fiber and may help prevent the development of cancer.

# Mother Earth's Essential Dressing

Yield: about 2 cups

**Mix** all the ingredients well. Keep stored in the refrigerator, and use on the Veggie Special and salads.

Per tablespoon: Calories: 97, Protein: 0 gm.,
     Fat: 10 gm., Carbohydrates: 0 gm.

1 cup olive oil

½ cup flax oil

¼ cup brown rice vinegar

3-4 cloves garlic, finely chopped

4 tablespoons fresh basil, finely
     chopped

shot of shoyu

¼ teaspoon Spike

1 teaspoon lemon juice

tarragon, parsley, and rosemary
     to taste

## Did you know?

Flax oil is an excellent source of omega-3 and omega-6 essential fatty acids. Essential fatty acids must be obtained from food sources. They enhance the body's immune system and play an important role in promoting normal growth. They have been shown to raise the levels of HDL (the good cholesterol) and lower LDL (the bad cholesterol). Signs of deficiency include dry skin, eczema, psoriasis, arthritis, acne, asthma, and prostate enlargement.

# Carrot and Sea Plant Salad

Serves 4 to 6

1 cup arame or hijiki sea
  vegetables

1 small onion, minced

2 cloves garlic, chopped in
  chunks

2 carrots, cut into matchsticks

¾ cup soaking water

1 tablespoon tamari

1 tablespoon mirin

**Place** the arame in a small mixing bowl, cover with water, and soak for about 10 minutes. Drain and reserve the water, discarding the sediment at the bottom.

**Place** a few drops of toasted sesame oil in a large skillet, bring to medium-high heat, add the onion and garlic, and sauté for 2 minutes.

**Add** the arame and carrots, and sauté 2 more minutes.

**Add** the soaking water and tamari to the vegetables, cover, and simmer on medium heat for about 20 minutes until most of the water is absorbed.

**Remove** the lid, add the mirin, turn off the heat, and serve warm or cold.

Per serving: Calories: 35, Protein: 1 gm., Fat: 0 gm.,
  Carbohydrates: 7 gm.

# Hijiki with Toasted Sesame Seeds

Yield: 2 cups

**Place** the hijiki in a medium-size mixing bowl. Cover with water, soak 5 minutes, drain, and chop. Save the cooking water for soup stock, discarding the sediment at the bottom.

**Roast** the sesame seeds in a dry skillet on medium-high heat for about 10 minutes (or in an oven at 350° for about 15 minutes) until the seeds give off a nutty aroma, stirring constantly. Be careful not to burn the seeds, and never leave them unattended. The seeds will start to fly all over the kitchen! Place the roasted seeds in a dish.

**Add** a few drops of toasted sesame oil to a hot skillet. Add the chopped hijiki and onions, and sauté for about 4 minutes.

**Stir** in the mirin, tamari, and rice syrup, and simmer on low for 15 minutes.

**Top** with the toasted sesame seeds, and serve hot or at room temperature.

Per cup: Calories: 115, Protein: 3 gm., Fat: 4 gm., Carbohydrates: 15 gm.

1 cup dried hijiki

4 tablespoons unhulled sesame seeds

2 onions, chopped

4 tablespoons mirin

2 tablespoons tamari

1 tablespoon rice syrup or honey

## Did you know?

While sea vegetables may appear costly, you're getting a lot more for your money because they expand. Hijiki expands to four times its original volume.

# Seasoned Greens

Serves 10

3 pounds kale or collards

3 tablespoons flax oil

3 tablespoons brown rice
  vinegar

2 tablespoons low-sodium soy
  sauce

1 teaspoon toasted sesame oil

2 tablespoons water

1½ teaspoons maple syrup

1 teaspoon roasted sesame
  seeds (optional)

**Thoroughly** wash and drain the kale.

**In a large pot**, steam the kale for approximately 15 minutes until tender.

**Remove** from the burner and allow to cool until the greens can be handled. Chop up the greens, including the stems. Discard some of the bigger and tougher stems.

**In a large mixing bowl**, mix together the flax oil, vinegar, soy sauce, sesame oil, water, and maple syrup.

**Mix** the chopped greens with the sesame vinaigrette, and garnish with sesame seeds. This can be served immediately while still warm, or it can be served cold or at room temperature.

Per serving: Calories: 114, Protein: 3 gm., Fat: 4 gm.,
  Carbohydrates: 14 gm.

**Variation:** For just one pound of greens use, 2 tablespoons flax oil, 1 tablespoon soy sauce, 1 tablespoon mirin, 2 tablespoons brown rice vinegar, and 1 teaspoon maple syrup.

## About this recipe—

This is a great way to enrich your diet with flax oil (which is rich in essential fatty acids) and greens (which are rich in beta carotene). The dark green, leafy vegetables also contain some omega-3 fatty acids.

## Did you know?

Kale and collards are both wonder foods; full of vitamin A, calcium, and iron. They are beneficial to the nervous system and the digestive system. Try and incorporate both of these greens into your diet weekly.

Flax seeds are the richest source of lignans. Plant lignans have been found to offer protection against cancer, particularly breast cancer. It is currently being recommended that women increase the amount of plant lignans in their diet.

# Seasoned Arame

Serves 4

**Place** the arame in a medium-size bowl, and cover with water. Allow to soak for about 15 minutes. Drain and reserve the soaking water for tea or soup stock. Discard the sediment at the bottom.

**Spray** a skillet with cooking oil or use a drop or two of toasted sesame oil to sauté the arame for a few minutes, and set aside.

**Mix** together the mirin, vinegar, and soy sauce.

**Place** the arame in a storage container, and add the dressing. Serve warm or cold. This is great as a side vegetable dish.

1 cup dry arame

1 tablespoon mirin

2 tablespoons brown rice vinegar

1-2 tablespoons soy sauce

Per serving: Calories: 22. Protein: 1 gm.. Fat: 0 gm.. Carbohydrates: 4 gm.

# Special Occasion Brunch

## Six-Layer Mexican Bean Dip

Serves 6

1 (15 oz.) can vegetarian refried
    beans

1 tablespoon taco seasoning

1 cup salsa

1 cup soy cheddar cheese,
    grated

2 cups Mock Guacamole (page
    32)

1 medium tomato, chopped

tofu sour cream (optional)

baked corn tortilla chips

**In a 12-inch pizza pan** or a 2-quart serving bowl, alternately layer the first four ingredients.

**Heat** or microwave to melt the cheese, and add the guacamole, tomato, and sour cream.

**Surround** the pizza with corn chip scoopers.

Per serving: Calories: 243, Protein: 10 gm., Fat: 3 gm.,
    Carbohydrates: 41 gm.

# Spinach Salad with Hot Miso Dressing

Serves 6 to 8

**Steam** the tempeh for 20 minutes. When it is cool, dice it into ½-inch cubes, and toast in a non-stick skillet for a few minutes until lightly browned.

**Wash** the spinach and lettuce well, taking care to rinse the undersides of the leaves. Discard the spinach stems. **Dry** and tear the leaves into a medium salad bowl.

**Add** the red onion, mushrooms, and green peas.

**Combine** the oil, hot water, brown rice syrup, miso, tamari, lemon juice, scallions, garlic, and cayenne in a blender. If the blended ingredients tend to separate, add a little more hot water. Toss gently with the salad, and serve at once.

Per serving: Calories: 241, Protein: 5 gm., Fat: 15 gm., Carbohydrates: 17 gm.

4 oz. tempeh

1 pound spinach

1 small head Romaine lettuce

1 small red onion, thinly sliced and separated into rings

4 oz. button mushrooms, washed and thinly sliced

½ cup frozen green peas, defrosted

¼ cup canola oil or flax oil

2 tablespoons hot water

¼ cup brown rice syrup or honey

2 tablespoons barley miso

2 tablespoons tamari

2 tablespoons fresh lemon juice

3 scallions

1 clove garlic

dash cayenne

## Did you know?

Mushrooms are a good source of germanium. Germanium is important because it increases the flow of oxygen to the body's cells, which in turn leads to a stronger immune system. Shiitake mushrooms help decrease cholesterol and fat in the blood. They also help the body eliminate excessive protein residues from the consumption of too much animal protein.

# Cream of Mushroom Soup

Serves 4

2 stalks celery, chopped

1 bunch green onions and
   tops, washed and chopped

¼ pound (2 cups) fresh
   mushrooms, chopped

1 teaspoon sesame oil

2 tablespoons whole wheat
   flour

3 cups plain soymilk

¼ teaspoon sea salt

⅛ teaspoon nutmeg

1 teaspoon tamari

**In a large soup pot**, sauté the celery, green onions, and mushrooms in the oil on medium-high heat for about 5 minutes until tender, stirring constantly.

**Lower** the heat to medium, and stir the flour in with the vegetables.

**Slowly add** the soymilk, then the spices, and tamari, stirring constantly. You may need to turn the heat up a bit to thicken. Continue to cook, stirring occasionally to thicken. Serve warm.

Per serving: Calories: 98, Protein: 5 gm., Fat: 5 gm., Carbohydrates: 8 gm.

## About this recipe——

When using the lite soymilk for the Cream of Mushroom Soup, increase the whole wheat flour by 1 tablespoon, and reduce the oil to one teaspoon.

## Food for thought . . .

"More die in the United States of too much food than too little,"

—John Kenneth Galbraith

# Cauliflower Pie with Grated Zucchini Crust

Serves 6 to 8

**Preheat** the oven to 400°.

**To make the crust,** place the zucchini, carrots, onions, and potatoes in a colander, sprinkle with ½ teaspoon salt, and let set for 10 minutes. Squeeze out the excess liquid, and place in a medium-size mixing bowl.

**Add** the egg replacer mixture, and mix well.

**Press** into the bottom and sides of an oiled 9-inch (or deep dish) pie pan.

**Pre-bake** the crust for 40 minutes until browned.

**Reduce** the oven to 375°.

**In a large skillet** sauté the onion and garlic in 2 tablespoons water for about 4 minutes.

**Add** the cauliflower, tarragon, basil, salt, black pepper, and 2 more tablespoons water, cover, and steam for about 10 minutes, stirring occasionally.

**Sprinkle** ½ cup of the soy cheese on the pre-baked crust.

**Spread** the vegetable mixture over the cheese.

**Sprinkle** the remaining cheese over the top.

**Mix** together the egg replacer, water, and rice or soymilk, and pour over the pie. Sprinkle the top with the paprika.

**Bake** for 40 minutes until firm.

Per serving: Calories: 136, Protein: 4 gm., Fat: 5 gm., Carbohydrates: 18 gm.

¼ cup zucchini, grated

½ cup carrots, grated

¼ cup onions, grated

2 cups potatoes, grated

½ teaspoon sea salt

1½ teaspoons egg replacer + 2 tablespoons water

1 small onion, chopped

2 cloves garlic, minced

3 cups cauliflower florettes

½ teaspoon tarragon

½ teaspoon basil

pinch of sea salt

pinch of black pepper

2 tablespoons water

1 cup soy cheddar cheese, grated

3 teaspoons egg replacer + 4 tablespoons water

¼ cup rice or soymilk

¼ teaspoon paprika

## Did you know?

Much of the calcium in cauliflower is found in the greens around the head. Instead of discarding these greens, try cooking with them.

# Broccoli and Red Pepper Sauté

Serves 4

1 teaspoon olive oil

2 teaspoons garlic, minced

½ head broccoli flowers and
  stems, chopped

½ red pepper, chopped

2 teaspoons tamari

**Place** the olive oil in a large skillet, turn the heat to medium-high, add the garlic, and sauté for 1 minute.

**Add** the broccoli and sauté 5 more minutes.

**Add** the red pepper and cook 3 more minutes until tender. The broccoli should be crisp-tender.

**Lower** the heat and pour the tamari over the broccoli mixture. Serve warm.

Per serving: Calories: 34, Protein: 1 gm., Fat: 1 gm.,
  Carbohydrates: 4 gm.

# Vanilla Cheesecake
# with Raspberry Sauce

Serves 12

**Prepare** the graham cracker crust in the Strawberry Kiwi Fruit Tart recipe (page 141). Press the crust into an oiled 10-inch spring form pan or pie plate, and bake at 375° for 7 minutes. Remove and cool.

**In a blender**, mix together the soymilk, tofu, and 1 cup maple syrup, adding the tofu a little at a time so that it blends smoothly.

**Add** the lemon juice, vanilla, almond extract, and salt to the blender mixture.

**Add** the bananas slowly by chunks, stopping the blender to stir with a wooden spoon to be sure the mixture is well blended.

**Slowly blend** in the tahini until well blended.

**Pour** the mixture into the prebaked pie crust. Bake in a 350° oven for 40 to 45 minutes until firm.

**Meanwhile**, puree the raspberries, and 1 tablespoon maple syrup in the blender, and strain through a fine sieve. Discard the raspberry seeds.

**Chill** the cheesecake before serving, and serve each piece with raspberry sauce.

Per serving: Calories: 209, Protein: 5 gm., Fat: 7 gm.,
    Carbohydrates: 31 gm.

1 graham cracker crust

½ cup vanilla soymilk

1 pound + 2 oz. firm tofu,
    drained

1 cup maple syrup

3 teaspoons lemon juice

1 teaspoon vanilla extract

¼ teaspoon almond extract

⅛ teaspoon sea salt

3 ripe bananas, cut in chunks

¼ cup tahini

2 cups frozen, unsweetened
    raspberries, thawed

1 tablespoon maple syrup

# Glossary

**Agar-Agar**—is a natural, vegetarian alternative to gelatin. It is made from seaweed and is a rich source of essential minerals. It can be used in desserts, jello, jellies, aspics, and fillings. It is available in flakes, powder, strands, or bars called kanten. It will set at room temperature in half an hour or more quickly if refrigerated. Agar will not set in the presence of acetic acid, found in wine and distilled vinegars. It also will not set with the high proportion of oxalic acid found in chocolate, spinach, and rhubarb.

**Amaranth**—was the sacred grain of the Aztecs. It is higher in protein than wheat or corn, and supplies all the essential amino acids to make it a complete protein. Unlike most grains, it is a good source of vitamin C. It is also a good source of iron and calcium. Because it is gluten-free, it's a good grain for people who are allergic to wheat.

**Arrowroot**—was used by the Indians to heal wounds made by poison arrows. It is a natural thickener. It is good for thickening sauces, gravies, and puddings. Arrowroot is a substitute for cornstarch and has more nutritive value. Be sure to mix the arrowroot with a little cold water before adding to sauce or gravy stock. After adding, stir constantly, bring to a boil, and lower the heat.

**Baking powder**—Buy aluminum-free baking powder, or make your own. For the equivalent of 1 teaspoon of baking powder in a recipe, use ⅝ teaspoon of cream of tarter and ¼ teaspoon of baking soda. To make sodium-free baking powder, mix ¼ cup cream of tarter, ¼ cup arrowroot, and 2 tablespoons of potassium bicarbonate (available in most pharmacies). Store in an air-tight container. Use in the same amounts as baking powder in any recipe.

**Baking Soda**—Potassium bicarbonate can be substituted for baking soda, and used to make sodium-free baking powder (see recipe under baking powder).

**Brown Rice**—is a whole grain rich in B vitamins and trace minerals and is particularly soothing to the nervous system and brain. It is considered the easiest grain to digest and is good for people with allergies. There are several varieties available, such as short-grain, medium-grain, long-grain, sweet brown, basmati, etc.

**Brown Rice Syrup**—is a natural sweetener made from rice. It is a healthy alternative to sugar. It is more slowly absorbed into the bloodstream and does not cause a drop in the blood sugar level like sugar.

**Brown Rice Vinegar**—is a naturally fermented vinegar made from brown rice. It does not deplete the body of minerals like distilled vinegar.

**Bulgur Wheat**—is a cracked wheat that has been partially boiled, dried, and ground. It is used to make tabouli, a popular Middle Eastern dish. It can be prepared just by adding water (usually boiling water) and soaking.

**Cilantro**—looks very much like, and is related to, parsley. It has a pungent, spicy flavor. Its seed, called coriander, is commonly found in spicy cuisines. It is known as Chinese parsley in the Orient and cilantro in Mexico.

**Carob**—is a natural alternative to chocolate. It comes from the pod or fruit of the carob tree. Unlike chocolate, it contains no theobromine, (a caffeine-like substance) or oxalic acid (which inhibits the absorption of calcium). It is available in powdered form or as carob chips. There are carob chips available that contain no dairy or sugar.

**Egg replacer**—is a powdered substitute for eggs. It contains no eggs and no preservatives or flavorings. Egg replacer provides structure in baked goods instead of using eggs. It can also be whipped and used as a substitution for egg whites.

**Flax Oil**—is a high quality, cold pressed, unrefined, unbleached oil that is free of trans-fatty acids. It is an excellent source of essential fatty acids. It is important not to heat flax oil because heat will destroy the important nutrients. It must be kept refrigerated to insure freshness. It is excellent as a base for salad dressings.

**Gingerroot**—is the pungent, knobby root of the tropical plant zingebar. A basic spice in all oriental cooking, the fresh root can be minced or grated. Wrapped tightly in plastic and kept in the refrigerator, one piece of root will last for weeks. It will keep for months in the freezer, and bits can be shaved off as needed.

**Mirin**—is a popular Japanese rice cooking wine that is a substitute for white cooking wine. Some varieties may have sugar or corn syrup added—look for the naturally brewed varieties. The alcohol content in the mirin evaporates quickly during cooking. Mirin has a sweet flavor and can be added to dressings, marinades, sauces, dips, soups, and stir frys.

**Miso**—is a creamy paste made from fermented soybeans and sea salt. It is a savory, high-protein seasoning and comes several of flavors. It is a natural alternative to bouillon. It has been a favorite of the Japanese for centuries. They use it as a flavoring, a digestive aid, and a health tonic. It should be kept refrigerated after opening.

**Nutritional Yeast**—is a protein-rich seasoning available in powder or flake form. The yeast is grown on a molasses base. It has a cheezy flavor and a yellow color. It is an excellent source of B vitamins (sometimes it is fortified with B12, as well as protein and essential amino acids).

**Quinoa (keen-wa)**—was a staple of the Incas. It is a complete-protein grain and therefore contains all the essential amino acids. It is also rich in fatty acids, vitamins, and minerals. Because it is gluten-free, it's a good grain for people who are allergic to wheat. It cooks up in only 15 minutes. Rinse quinoa before cooking to remove a bitter resin that coats the seeds.

**Rice Milk**—is a non-dairy, cholesterol-free, lactose-free, and soy-free milk made from rice. It has the consistency of skim milk and can be used in equivalent proportions. It can be substituted for cow or soymilk. It is now available fortified with vitamins, A and D and calcium. It is low in fat.

**Sea Salt**—is salt evaporated from sea water and is rich in the trace minerals that common table salt lacks.

**Sea Vegetables**—offer a powerhouse of nutritional value. Edible seaweed comes in a variety of forms. They are the best vegetable source of iodine and are rich in vitamins A, E, and the B vitamins. Some seaweed even has B12. Sea vegetables also contain calcium, other minerals, and protein. They help promote the proper functioning of the thyroid gland, and help cleanse the body of fats. Varieties include; agar agar (used for its jelling properties); nori (used for sushi); wakame (traditionally used in miso soup); kombu (used in cooking beans); dulse (used as a condiment or chopped and added to salads); The darker sea vegetables, hijiki and arame, have been used to help remove radioactive strontium-90 from the body.

**Seitan**—(also called wheat meat) is an alternative to meat. It is made from wheat gluten. It is a protein rich food which somewhat resembles meat in appearance and texture. It can be used for stir frys, stuffings, fajitas, and more. It can be purchased fresh in tubs, canned, frozen, or boxed as a dry powder that has to be prepared.

**Soy Cheese**—is a non-dairy, cholesterol-free, and lactose-free cheese made from soybeans. Most of the firmer soy cheeses, that have the ability to melt just like regular cheese, do contain casein (a milk protein) and should be avoided by those who are allergic to casein. There are, however, lactose-free and casein-free varieties available.

**Soymilk**—is a non-dairy, cholesterol-free milk made from soybeans. It is a great alternative to cow's milk for those who are lactose intolerant. It can be substituted in any recipe that calls for milk. It is available in natural foods stores, and some supermarkets are now carrying soymilk either fresh in the dairy case or in aseptic cartons that will keep unrefrigerated for about 12 months, unopened. Soymilk is not recommended for very young babies. It doesn't have the right balance of casein, milk sugars, and other carbohydrates to be properly assimilated by an infant. It is also available fortified with vitamins A and D and calcium and also in reduced-fat versions.

**Soy Sauce**—is a salty food flavoring that is available in two varieties in the natural foods stores. Shoyu is made from soybeans, cracked wheat, and sea salt. Shoyu should only be added to foods during the last few minutes of cooking as the evaporation of its alcohol destroys its rich flavor and aroma. Tamari is made without the wheat and is very heat stable (it will not flash off during high heat). The advantage of using naturally brewed soy sauce (which means aging for one to two years) over pure salt in seasoning foods is that you are also getting a naturally fermented vegetable protein in the form of 18 amino acids. (Soy sauce contains about 20% salt). You can use less tamari than pure salt to get the same level of seasoning. The synthetic soy sauce usually sold in supermarkets is made very quickly, and may contain corn syrup, caramel coloring, hydrolyzed vegetable protein, hydrochloric acid, and salt.

**Toasted Sesame Oil**—is a dark, delicious, nutty-flavored oil that is good for stir-frying, sauces, marinades, and dressings. It is frequently used in Oriental cooking.

**Tofu**—also known as bean curd in the Orient, is a bland, custard-like product made by curdling soymilk. It comes in a block form, in three consistencies—soft, firm, and extra-firm. It is cholesterol-free, low calorie, and contains calcium. It is usually sold prepackaged in a plastic tub covered with water and should be kept covered with water in the refrigerator after being opened. Unopened, aseptic tofu has a shelf life of one year. Tofu can be used to make dips, dressings, desserts, stir frys, and much much more.

**Tempeh**—is a fermented soybean cake made by natural culturing, similar to that used to make cheese, yogurt, and sourdough. It originated in Indonesia where it is the main protein staple. It has the highest quality protein of all the soyfoods. It is high in fiber, cholesterol-free, and contains natural antibiotics that safeguard the intestinal tract. It is a good substitute for meat in the diet. Tempeh can be made from other beans, grains, and seeds. Some varieties mix in vegetables and sea vegetables. Always steam or cook your tempeh for 20 minutes before eating or preparing. Never eat it raw.

**Udon**—are thick Japanese noodles made from wheat flour.

**Umeboshi Vinegar**—is the juice left over after pickling the umeboshi plum. The umeboshi plum is a variety of apricot pickled in red shiso leaves. The vinegar is very strong, salty, and tart so use it sparingly. Umeboshi is a great antacid due to its high alkaline content and is high in vitamin C.

**Wasabi**—is the green Japanese horse-radish familiar to sushi eaters. It is available as a powder or a paste. It is very hot, so be sure to use it sparingly. Wasabi is rich in digestive enzymes. You can mix it with soy sauce as a dipping sauce.

**Wheat Berries**—are unground kernels of wheat that are excellent for sprouting or cooking whole.

**Whole Wheat Pastry Flour**—is made from the whole grain of soft wheat. It is low in gluten, and makes a light pastry dough which is great for baked goods. It contains all the vitamins and minerals of whole wheat flour, which is usually made from hard winter wheat.

# *Appendix*
## *Natural Foods Substitutions*

| Food | Amount | Substitution |
|---|---|---|
| Baking powder | 1 teaspoon | ¼ tsp. baking soda + ½ tsp. cream of tartar |
| Baking soda | 1 teaspoon | ½ tsp. baking soda + 1½ tsp. lemon juice |
| Beans, canned | 15 to 16 oz | 2 cups home cooked (1 cup dried) |
| Bran | ¾ cup | ¼ cup flour (for muffins and cupcakes) |
| | 1 cup | ¼ cup whole grain flour (whole grain breads) |
| Butter | 1 cup | ⅞ cup oil + 3 Tbsp. liquid |
| | 1 cup | 1 cup corn oil + ½ tsp. sea salt |
| | 1 cup in baking | 1 cup Prune Puree (page 136) |
| | 1 cup in baking | 1 cup applesauce |
| Buttermilk | 1 cup | 1 cup soymilk + 1½ Tbsp. vinegar or lemon juice |
| Cheeses | soy equivalent | (available in mozzarella, cheddar, jalapeño, Monterey Jack) |
|   cottage cheese | ½ cup | ½ cup mashed tofu |
|   cream cheese | | Tofu Cream Cheese (page 34) |
|   sour cream | | soy sour cream |
| Cocoa | 1½ cups | 1 cup carob powder, or ¾ cup carob powder + ¼ cup coffee substitute |
| Chocolate (baking) | 1 square | 3 Tbsp. carob powder + 1 Tbsp. oil + 1 Tbsp. water + 1 Tbsp. coffee substitute |
| Coffee | | grain coffee substitute |
| Cornstarch | 1 Tablespoon | 1 Tbsp. arrowroot powder, 1 Tbsp. kudzu powder, 2 Tbsp. flour, or 1 Tbsp. tapioca |
| Cream, heavy | ¼ cup | 1 Tbsp. tahini dissolved in ¼ cup water |
| Cream, light | ¼ cup | ¼ cup low-fat soymilk thickened w/ 1 Tbsp. arrowroot |

| Food | Amount | Substitution |
|---|---|---|
| Egg | 1 | 1½ tsp. egg replacer + 2 Tbsp. water |
| Egg for leavening | | 1 Tbsp. arrowroot + 1 Tbsp. whole wheat flour + 2 Tbsp. water + ½ tsp. tahini, or 1 tsp. baking powder, or ½ teaspoon arrowroot + ¼ tsp. baking soda |
| Egg yolk | 1 | 1½ tsp. egg replacer + 1 Tbsp. water |
| Egg & yolk | 1 + 1 | 3 Tbsp. whole wheat pastry flour + 3 Tbsp. water + 1½ tsp. baking powder + 2 tsp. canola oil |
| Egg in baking as a binder | | 1 Tbsp. flaxseed + 3 Tbsp. water, or ¼ cup mashed tofu (the tofu must first be blended with water), or ½ ripe banana (for muffins and cookies), or 1 whole banana (for pancakes and cakes), or 1 Tbsp. defatted soy flour, or 1 Tbsp. powdered soy lecithin + 1 Tbsp. water, or 2 Tbsp. Arrowroot or cornstarch |
| Egg binder and leavener | | 4 Tbsp. cashew or almond butter + 2 Tbsp. lemon juice |
| Flour, white | 1 cup | 1 cup whole wheat pastry flour, or 1 cup whole wheat flour minus 2 Tbsp., or 1 cup white wheat flour (King Arthur brand) |
| Gelatin | 1 Tablespoon | 1 Tbsp. kanten flakes |
| Gelatin for 2 cups liquid | 4 tsp. | 2 tsp agar powder, or 4 Tbsp. agar flakes |
| Garlic, fresh | 1 clove | ½ tsp. garlic powder, or 1 tsp. minced garlic, or ⅓ tsp. crushed garlic |
| Herbs, fresh | 1 Tbsp. | 1 tsp. dried herb |
| Lemon juice | 1 cup | 6 regular lemons, juiced |
| | ¼ cup | 1 large lemon, juiced |
| Liquor (in recipes) | 1 Tbsp. | 1 tsp. natural liquor flavoring |
| Milk | 1 cup | 1 cup soymilk, or 1 cup cashew or almond nut milk |
| Mustard | 1 Tbsp. wet | 1 tsp. dried |
| Onion, raw | 1 medium | 1 Tbsp. dried flakes |
| Orange juice | ½ cup | 1 orange, juiced |

| Food | Amount | Substitution |
|------|--------|--------------|
| Salt | ½ teaspoon | ½ tsp. sea salt, or 1 Tbsp. miso, or 2 Tbsp. tamari |
| Shortening | 1 cup | ⅔ cup oil, or 1 cup soy margarine, or 1 cup applesauce, or 1 cup Prune Puree (page 136) |
| Soy sauce | 1 teaspoon | 1 tsp. shoyu, or ½ tsp. tamari |
| Spelt flour | 1 cup | 1 cup whole wheat flour |
| | 2½ cups | 2 cups all purpose flour |
| Sugar | ½ cup | *½ cup honey, or ⅓ cup molasses, or ½ cup maple syrup, or 1½ cups rice syrup, or 1½ cups barley malt, or ½ cup fruit concentrate. or 2 cups apple juice, or 1 cup apple butter |
| | | *When replacing sugar with a concentrated sweetener, like honey, molasses, maple syrup, etc., reduce the liquid in the recipe by ¼ cup. If the recipe uses no liquid, then for each ¾ cup concentrated sweetener used add 4 tablespoons flour. When using a concentrated sweetener; heat before using, and oil the measuring cup and spoon. Use more dry ingredients when using rice syrup and barley malt. |
| Vanilla extract | 1 tsp. | 1 inch vanilla bean |
| Vinegar, white, distilled | 1 Tbsp. | 1 Tbsp. brown rice, or apple cider, or umeboshi & balsamic vinegar |
| | ½ tsp. | 1 tsp. lemon juice |
| Water chestnuts | ½ cup | ½ cup chopped jicama, or ½ cup chopped Jerusalem artichoke |
| Wheat flour flour, | 1 cup | ¾ cup potato flour, or ¾ cup brown rice or ½ cup arrowroot + ½ cup soy flour, or 1 cup spelt flour, or 1 cup corn flour, or 1¼ cups barley flour, or 1⅓ cups oat or soy flour |
| White cooking wine | 1 Tbsp. | 1 Tbsp. mirin |
| Yogurt | 1 cup | 1 cup soy yogurt |

# Index

# BOOK PUBLISHING COMPANY

*since 1974—books that educate, inspire, and empower*

To find your favorite vegetarian and soyfood products online,
visit: www.healthy-eating.com

### Kids Can Cook
Dorothy Bates
978-1-57067-086-2
$ 12.95

### Simple Treats
Ellen Abraham
978-1-57067-137-1
$ 14.95

### The Simple Little Vegan
Slow Cooker
Michelle Rivera
978-1-57067-171-5
$ 9.95

### Muchie Madness
Dorothy Bates, Bobbie
Hinman, Robert Oser
978-1-57067-115-9
$ 9.95

### Vegan Vittles
Second Helpings
Jo Stepaniak
978-1-57067-200-2
$ 19.95

### Tofu Quick & Easy
Louise Hagler
978-1-57067-112-8
$ 12.95

Purchase these health titles and cookbooks from your local bookstore or
natural food store, or you can buy them directly from:

Book Publishing Company • P.O. Box 99 • Summertown, TN 38483    1-800-695-2241

*Please include $3.95 per book for shipping and handling.*